VOICES

IN YOUR

BLOOD

VOICES

Discovering Identity

IN YOUR

through Family History

BLOOD

by G.G. Vandagriff

ANDREWS

AND McMEEL

A Universal Press Syndicate Company

Kansas City

Voices in Your Blood: Discovering Identity Through Family History
Copyright © 1993 by G.G. Vandagriff.
For information write
Andrews and McMeel, a Universal Press Syndicate Company,
4900 Main Street, Kansas City,
Missouri 64112.

Library of Congress Cataloging-in-Publication Data

Vandagriff, G.G.
    Voices in your blood : discovering identity through family history
/ by G.G. Vandagriff
        p.   cm.
    Includes bibliographical references.
    ISBN 0-8362-8020-2 : $9.95
    1. Genealogy—Methodology.   2. United States—Genealogy—
Methodology.   I. Title.
CS9.V36   1993
929'.1—dc20   93-9782
                                                              CIP

First Printing, June 1993
Fourth Printing, December 1997

DEDICATED TO

MARY WILLIAMS

TOMBLIN

Who gave me her vision

AND TO DR. THAD

BILLINGSLEY

Who showed me my strength

Contents

Introduction

I like Alice Walker's description of family history. She said, ". . . love is the ladder that reaches through time: sometimes the first rung of this ladder is disguised, but that is only a test."

Excavating our own ladder of love rung by rung is an adventure akin to solving a mystery. The mystery is ourselves. Who are we underneath all the "shoulds" and the "musts"? Why do we accept certain things in our lives as "givens"? Why are our tastes and aspirations what they are? Where did we derive the pattern by which we have chosen to live?

Undertaking this quest into our genesis will lead us further and further into the reaches of history. There lies a heritage, oftentimes completely unexpected.

Not only are we influenced behaviorally and genetically by our forebears, but research described by Dr. Lewis Thomas in *The Lives of a Cell* has revealed the astounding fact that, in a very real way, we carry pieces of our ancestors within us. Microorganisms called mitochondria have been with us since we were eggs in our mothers' bodies. Those same microorganisms lived in our grandmothers, our great-grandmothers, and all the grandmothers before them. As this egg was fertilized by sperm from our fathers carrying their own mitochondria, our identity was forged and we grew into human beings. These bacterialike organisms stayed with us, performing the important function of helping our cells to breathe. As Dr. Thomas says, "There is the whole question of my identity . . . I have not, in a real sense, descended [from my ancestors] at all. I have brought them all along with me, or perhaps they have brought me."

What does this mean? It means that part of what is now me may actually have been with William the Conqueror at the Battle of Hastings. Something in me may have helped my great-grandmother as she toiled on the banks of the Volga River in Russia, hauling water in buckets suspended from a pole across her shoulders. When I read about the *Mayflower*, the revolutionary war, the westward migration, I am compelled to realize that *part of me may literally have been there.* What knowledge, what undiscovered heritage still lies latent within me?

And what about genetic memory? Is there such a thing? I can make a strong case for it. Twenty-five years ago, long before I became interested in family history, I lived in Austria as a student. As part of our course work, we traveled to Poland. We saw a Warsaw that had been leveled and rebuilt in the style of Soviet Socialist Realism—uninspired blocks of white plaster. The weather was gray, and our food consisted almost solely of ham and potatoes. Compared to Vienna, Paris, and London, Warsaw and the Polish countryside had little glamour. Yet, something inside of me awoke during that journey. All my senses came alive, and my curiosity ran rampant, keeping me awake at night. I needed to know how such a country had come to be crushed, and how such a people could still burn with that perceptible glow of Polish individuality. I didn't feel these stirrings in Hungary, Czechoslovakia, or Yugoslavia. Only in Poland.

An international-relations major, I had yet to choose my geographical area of concentration. When I returned home to Stanford, I flung myself headlong into the study of Polish history, Polish culture, Polish economics, and Polish politics. This led inevitably to a study of the Soviet Union, for which I grew to have a like fascination. I studied Russian literature, Russian history, even Russian cooking. I became an assistant editor for the *Yearbook of International Communist Affairs*, writing the profile on Poland for the 1970 edition.

Later, I attended graduate school to further my knowledge of Eastern European and Russian history. The only nonémigré in my department, I studied Polish and Soviet affairs with a ferocity amusing to my adviser, a survivor of Stalin's labor camps. Still I had no clue as to why I had been so obsessed by this seemingly grim quarter of the world.

Within months of receiving my master's degree, I began researching my own family history. Knowing vaguely that my mother's father and my father's mother were German, I assumed that I was half German.

Upon investigation, I found out that my mother's Germans had lived for 150 years in Russia, and my father's Germans were from a part of Prussia that is now Poland! The coincidence with my passion for these two unlikely places was surely too bizarre to be chance.

It gets better. Only recently, I have located the village church records on my father's ancestors. They were Prussians living in Pomerania who actually intermarried with Polish Lutherans. My third great-grandmother was Dorothea Sophia Polenska, a Polish name if ever there was one. I am now convinced that when I visited that country all those years ago, my Polish mitochondria woke up, quivering to attention. Perhaps it was the smell of all that ham!

Today's world offers poor soil for rooting. Families are parted by dysfunction and distance. Television and air travel are making us a homogenous nation, erasing regional differences, so that heritage is a lost and forgotten thing. The extended family is all but gone, and the nuclear family is in peril.

The tremendous impact of Alex Haley's *Roots* shows that we are a people hungry for our past, for our identity. Dorothy Spruill Redford was inspired by Haley to begin an intensive search for her own history. Like other blacks, she had passed through many phases in her identity crisis. Then came *Roots*, and ". . . it all rushed back, feelings I hadn't faced in years. Emptiness, anger, confusion, denial—most of all, denial."

Redford began with what she knew and painstakingly traced her slave ancestors (sometimes through bills of sale) back to a North Carolina plantation called Somerset. Not content to find her own ancestors, she traced all the descendants of the slaves at Somerset and organized a vast reunion.

The homecoming aroused tremendous emotion and an unexpected healing. Senator Clarence Blount, age sixty-five, is quoted by Redford: "'I suppose there is still embarrassment,' he said, of any reminders of slavery. 'I'm sure our country is embarrassed. But we don't feel embarrassment here. Think about the strength it took to build this place. Talk about true grit; talk about the right stuff. They had it—and so do we.'"

Discovering your heritage is a homecoming in the truest sense. The entity that we call "me" is the most recent chapter in a long line of stories—the stories belonging to those who make up our pedigree. Our ancestors have met life's challenges in their own particular ways, and in doing so have bequeathed to each of us a uniquely individual heritage. Part of that heritage contains burdens that are difficult and part of it contains our richest blessings. This tale gives us a place in history, a place in the universe. It is, to the fragmented, angst-ridden soul, the balm of Gilead.

Referring to the tremendous success of her book *The Joy Luck Club*, Chinese-American author Amy Tan was asked by an interviewer, "I wonder if you think that the book's success in this country has something to do with the fact that many people here have a history that they are ignoring and would like to be in touch with more?" Tan replied, "I think that's partly true. The strongest reason, I think, is that I'm a baby boomer . . . and I think I wrote about something that hit a lot of baby boomer women whose mothers have either just recently died or may die in the near future."

The Joy Luck Club is a magnificent evocation of the Chinese heritage carried within a group of four women who lived through the twentieth-century tumult in China before coming to America and raising American daughters. The daughters, caught up in the newer culture, cannot and will not relate to the world left behind by their mothers. The reader is left with a tragic picture of an entire world lost.

Americans have the richest, most varied culture in the world. We cannot afford to lose it. It is our strength. We bring to each crisis and problem viewpoints as varied as the history of all the nationalities who have made their way to our shores. That history is not only the *Mayflower* and the revolutionary war. It is the history of mankind.

We all have a past. Down through the ages there was love, a love between people of different places, different tongues, and different times. That love ultimately created the person that is you.

Every name on your pedigree tells a different story. You have thousands of stories in you. What are they? Let's find out.

ONE

Your Missing Heritage

> Thus not only does democracy make every man forget his ancestors, but it hides his descendants and separates his contemporaries from him; it throws him back forever upon himself alone and threatens in the end to confine him entirely within the solitude of his own heart.
> —Alexis de Toqueville, *Democracy in America*

During the four hundred years of our existence as a melting pot, the people of this continent have created a new nationality—the American. Being "American" has meant different things to different people at different times.

I grew up in the post–World War II era. In the fifties, especially in Southern California where I lived, the term American meant red, white, and blue, but not black, brown, and yellow. American was not so much what you *were* as what you were *not*. There was a vacuum where positive identity should have been.

In my upper-middle-class suburb, being alike was the main goal. I was blond, blue-eyed, and freckled. As the years advanced, I had orthodontia to create the perfect smile, frosted my hair to keep it blond, got contact lenses, and spent weeks in the sun getting a California tan. I looked like all the other "California Girls" the Beach Boys sang about, lying in a perfect row on the sand like so many herrings in a fish shop.

A "California Girl" didn't have much identity. She thought like everyone else her age, and if she looked the least bit different (as I did with my Prussian nose) it was a great source of anguish. In those days, it was even some sort of sin to be left-handed. Told that he lived in a right-handed world and would have to conform to it, my husband had the pencil literally taken out of his left hand by his first-grade teacher.

Part of being American was our air-raid drills at school and propaganda films on the Red Menace. We trembled through the Cuban missile crisis, wondering whether Russia would destroy us as it promised. We heard clashing sounds like sabers rattling when the wall went up in Berlin. In the American frame of reference, there was no place for being Russian, Prussian, or Chinese. Either you were an American or you weren't. People did not talk about their heritage unless they had a DAR pedigree. It just wasn't done.

Not until I went to study in Austria did I come face-to-face with the question of my identity. For the first time, surrounded by a foreign, and in many ways hostile, culture, I had to ask myself, "What does it mean to be an American?" "Who am I, really?"

When I visited the Auschwitz concentration camp, I felt my own share of war guilt as a Christian. What did it mean to be a Christian in a world where such atrocities were permitted? With me were many Jewish friends who found themselves reliving the nightmare that their spiritual kin had endured only two decades before. For them, being Jewish took on new meaning, and the world would never look the same again.

I suppose I could sum up this entire discussion by saying that I came of age in the sixties. Baby boomers from all over the country have shared this experience to some degree and can sympathize with my identity crisis. But I have learned that in some sense each generation has had its own wilderness to conquer, its own mark to make. My parents came of age during the depression, their parents during World War I, and so on.

Searching my background and foreground for clues as to who I was and what I believed, I scrutinized my values, my core beliefs. I went back to Stanford with a new assertiveness. I wasn't a "California Girl" any longer, but I wasn't certain who I was. I began listening eagerly to ideas, to people, collecting opinions and running them through my neophyte belief structure. I began to take an interest in my parents and grandparents as people. They were no longer simply appendages to me, but individuals with passions and problems. Why were they the way they were? Why had they made the choices they had? I had never stopped to wonder.

These questions eventually led me to the great passion of my life, family history. There I truly found myself. I do not have a monolithic identity, but rather I am myself a melting pot, bubbling with passions. Every new ancestor I find brings a new contribution to the pot, a special spice and flavor. To embrace my heritage is to enter a timeless dimension peopled by new fathers and mothers to whom I am connected by love. Though I have never known these people, I am a part of their posterity, and they have left a rich inheritance for me. In order to claim the inheritance, I must participate in a sort of treasure hunt, first finding them, and then finding out about them. As I see my own traits in my ancestors, different facets of these traits, both positive and negative, are illuminated. They have left lessons for me in the living of their lives.

Perhaps the most important thing that happens to us when we claim our lost heritage is that we gain unique perspective; we begin to understand what it is to be human, what it is to live a life where we learn from experiences—grief, shame, sorrow, pain, joy, success, pride, and triumph. Entering into our ancestors' emotions, by proxy as it were, we grow in charity and self-knowledge, and lessen in fear.

Richard Llewellyn expressed this truth most poignantly in his classic, *How Green Was My Valley*:

> Courage came to me from the height of the mountain, and with it came the dignity of manhood, and knowledge of the Tree of Life, for now I was a branch, running with the vital blood, waiting in the darkness of the Garden for some unknown Eve to tempt me with the apple of her beauty, that we might know our nakedness, and bring forth sons and daughters to magnify the Lord our God.
>
> I saw behind me those who had gone, and before me, those who are to come. I looked back and saw my father, and his father, and all our fathers, and in front, to see my son, and his son, and the sons upon sons beyond.
>
> And their eyes were my eyes.
>
> As I felt, so they had felt, and were to feel, as then, so now, as tomorrow and forever. Then I was not afraid, for I was in a long line that had no beginning, and no end, and the hand of his father grasped my father's hand, and his hand was in mine, and my unborn son took my right hand, and all, up and down the line that stretched from Time That Was, to Time That Is, and Is Not Yet, raised their hands to show the link, and we found that we were one, born of Woman, Son of Man, made in the Image, fashioned in the Womb by the Will of God, the Eternal Father.

You have a place in this eternal chain. You can connect yourself to the past that lies within you.

How? You begin by asking questions.

TWO

Asking Questions

Where are Uncle Isaac and Aunt Emily,
And old Towny Kincaid and Sevigne Houghton,
And Major Walker who had talked
With venerable men of the revolution?—
All, all, are sleeping on the hill. . . .
—Edgar Lee Masters, *Spoon River Anthology*

Quizzing Your Relatives

In his *Spoon River Anthology*, Edgar Lee Masters gives voices to the dead of the Spoon River Cemetery. Each of the people buried there recites his or her own epitaph. Unfortunately, our dead aren't so eloquent, but the next best thing to hearing them speak is to talk to your relatives who knew them or heard stories about them. It is imperative that you tap the memories of those relatives before they join the others who are sleeping on the hill.

Alex Haley collected the bulk of the material for *Roots* almost by osmosis when, as a small boy, he sat unnoticed on the porch, listening to his grandmother and her sisters talk about the "old days." Long after they were dead, he conceived of the idea for his book, and wished he had written all the stories down when he was young. He had, of course, had no idea how important they would one day be to him.

If possible, you should interview each living relative—parents, grandparents, aunts, uncles, cousins—either over the telephone or in person. This may sound a little formal, but it is amazing how much we store in our memories that we don't even realize is there. Planned questions may elicit a surprising wealth of information.

Following are some sample questions that you can use to jump start your interviews.

1. Birth date and birthplace?
2. Marriage date and place?
3. All residences, with dates?

4

4. Education?
5. Employment?
6. Military service?
7. Earliest memories of relatives—aunts, uncles, grandparents, cousins?
8. Can you construct a pedigree, going back as far as you can?
9. Where do your aunts, uncles, and cousins live? Do you have addresses?
10. Family traditions—what can you tell me about your parents? What were you told about your ancestors? Where did they come from? Did they immigrate? Did they fight in any wars? Where are they buried? Do you remember being shown any photographs of them? If so, who has them now? Are there others in the family interested in the family history? If so, how can I get in touch with them?
11. Do you have any old photographs, obituaries, letters, or scrapbooks?
12. How did you meet your husband/wife? What was your courtship like?
13. What is your happiest/funniest/saddest memory?
14. What strikes you as the greatest difference in the childhood of today's youngsters compared to what you experienced as a child?
15. What were holidays like?
16. What special foods did you enjoy?
17. What were your hobbies as a child, teenager, young adult?
18. What were your dreams and aspirations?

Some of these questions may not be tactful under certain circumstances. You can, of course, be the judge. My experience is that once you get your relatives talking, the memories begin to flow fairly easily.

If possible, consider audio- or videotaping your live interviews. Not only does this free you from the necessity of taking notes, but it gives you an enduring record, an oral history that may be very valuable to future generations. I audio-taped a long interview with my father's mother several years before she passed away. She was German and had always seemed the soul of propriety to me. When I began asking her about her courtship, she started giggling like a schoolgirl. My mind absolutely boggled at the fact that she had eloped with my grandfather!

After her death, I transcribed the interview and gave it to my father for Christmas. It meant a great deal to him, for there were many little details in it that he had never known. (I don't think he knew she eloped either.)

Gathering information from the living needn't be a time-consuming task. It can be done in small blocks of time. Take ten minutes to make a phone call to a distant relative. Such family members will be pleased to hear from you, and if they are elderly, will be happy to find someone who is interested in them and their past.

I cannot overemphasize the importance of starting this work without delay. Through the French Family Association surname exchange, I found a distant cousin who was also descended from Adolphus French, an ancestor I had just discovered. When I called her home, her husband told me she was in a nursing home. Suffering from congestive heart failure, she found speech difficult, but he knew she would want to talk to me, so he arranged for us to speak to one another. We had a short conversation where she discussed her unrealized hopes concerning her research, and she expressed the wish that I would be able to solve the Adolphus French puzzle. She was very ill, but promised me that upon her death, I could have all her records. She had spent a lifetime gathering them and had no children. *She died within the week.*

Her husband sent me two books, including the records of my fourth great-grandfather,* Adolphus French, and his *fifteen children.* This information had been passed down to my cousin from Adolphus's thirteenth child, who had written it on the back of a laundry ledger kept during the Civil War. It gave me birth and death dates for Adolphus and his wife, her maiden name (Grinnell), and the birth dates of all the children. There is no record anywhere else of this family, for they settled in the raw wilderness of western New York. There are no church or civil records from the period. If I hadn't telephoned, my cousin's husband would have thrown these precious facts away along with the rest of her genealogy.

I must add a word of caution about family traditions and the memories of relatives. Like all witnesses, your relatives' memories are fallible. They may have heard some stories second- or thirdhand. Each

*In genealogical parlance, "fourth great-grandfather" means "great-great-great-great grandfather"; "fourth" refers to the number of "greats." This shorthand will appear throughout the book.

generation tends to add a bit of color to the family tree. I am still looking for the "Indian blood" I am supposed to have.

Questioning the "Givens"

Where possible, document everything you can. You must keep in mind that secondary evidence, any evidence that is not taken from a primary source (i.e., vital records), may be in error.

In other words, keep an open mind. Evidence may conflict. But if you persevere, the truth will out! There is only one path to the next generation, and by following up your clues, you will find it eventually, no matter how many red herrings are laid across your path.

The place to start documentation is with yourself. How do you know when and where you were born and who your parents were? Do you have a birth certificate? If not, send for one. Appendix A at the back of the book tells where to send for vital records (birth, marriage, death, divorce) in the United States.

You probably won't find any surprises, but sometimes people do. A close friend of mine was hunting through a chest in her grandmother's house. Unexpectedly, she found a divorce decree ending the marriage between her mother and another man she had never known. When she looked at the date, the room seemed to go upside down. The unheard-of man had to be her father!

The man she had known as her father had adopted her in her infancy, and she had been issued a new birth certificate with his name on it. Her parents had never wanted her to know about her biological father. A reexamination of her birth certificate disclosed that it was issued after she was six years old.

For reasons such as this, we may run into opposition from some family members when we announce we are going to do genealogy. If you are determined, however, you will succeed. It may require tact, discretion, and some circuitous detective work, but you will succeed. Take comfort in the fact that almost every family has at least one skeleton in the closet. Everything we find is a clue to who we are, even the things no one wants us to know.

Illustration 2.1 shows a sample format for a letter requesting documents for either yourself or your ancestors. It is always a good idea when sending any kind of genealogy correspondence to include a self-addressed stamped envelope.

```
                                      Your Name
                                      Your Address

Date

Vital Records Section
Colorado Department of Health
4210 East 11th Avenue
Denver, Colorado 80220

Dear Sir or Madam:

I am compiling a family history and would like the death record
for my 3rd Great Grandmother, VIRA ANN BARBER who died 9 November
1900 in Fruita, Mesa County, Colorado.

Enclosed is a money order in the amount of $6.00.  Thank you very
much for your attention to this matter.

Sincerely,


Enclosures:  Check, Self-Addressed Stamped Envelope.
```

Illustration 2.1

Some states may have special requirements; for example, Arizona requires that your letter be notarized by a notary public for purposes of absolute identification. Any special requirements by the various states have been detailed in Appendix A.

After assembling all the records on yourself, begin gathering records and information on your parents and grandparents. Do not be contented with their word; send for the documentation. It is remarkable how little people sometimes know about their own origins. My grandmother celebrated her birthday on the wrong day her whole life long. My grandfather could never get a birth certificate, but was always told by his parents that he was born in Denver, Colorado. After he died, we found out from his stepmother that he had been born in Russia, but his father had never wanted him to know!

Vital records, if correct, can yield a surprising amount of information. Illustrations 2.2 and 2.3 show the marriage record of my great-grandparents, Augusta Raasch and Valentine Boos. Look carefully. What would a detective deduce from such a juicy piece of evidence? By applying his famous magnifying glass, Sherlock Holmes would decipher the bad copy and discover that the couple were married in Brooklyn by pastor Franz Koerner of the Evangelical Lutheran Church on February 17, 1883. (Interesting, considering that the groom came from a long line of German Catholics.) Witnesses to the wedding were H. Raasch, John Peley, and Anna Peley.

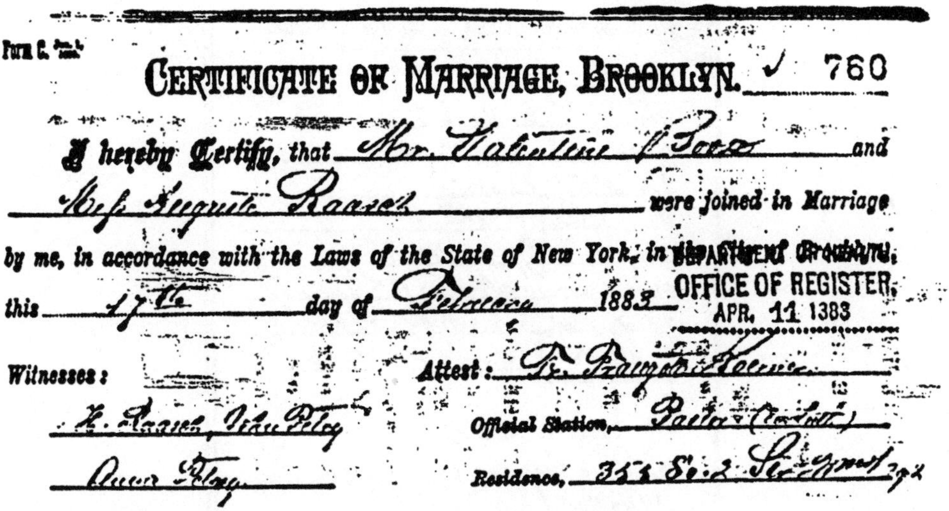
Form C.

CERTIFICATE OF MARRIAGE, BROOKLYN. ✓ 760

I hereby Certify, that ______ and ______ were joined in Marriage by me, in accordance with the Laws of the State of New York, in the ______

this 17th day of ______ 1883

OFFICE OF REGISTER, APR. 11 1383

Witnesses: Attest:

Official Station, Pastor

Residence,

Illustration 2.2

Now for the information on the second page: the groom's address is rather illegible, but certainly local. This is of importance to me, as I never knew that he resided in Brooklyn at all. Upon immigrating from Germany, he must have come to New York and settled in the German community in Brooklyn, where he met my great-grandmother. He was twenty-five years old, which means he was born sometime between February 17, 1857 and February 17, 1858. He claimed this to be his first marriage, and he was born in Mainz, Germany, to Jacob Boos and Anna Eberhard. (German records are wonderful—they invariably designate the wife by her maiden name!) Also interesting is his occupation: typesetter. This placed him in an enviable position among other immigrants, for he had a trade that he could practice in an urban setting in America.

I was particularly excited about the information on the bride, for almost all of it was news to me. Augusta lived locally also, at 722 Flushing Avenue, and was twenty-one. This places her birth date between February 17, 1861, and February 17, 1862. Her place of birth is less informative; she merely lists it as Pommern (Pommerania), which was a province in Prussia, now Poland. Her parents' names were Heinrich Raasch and Florentine Werth.

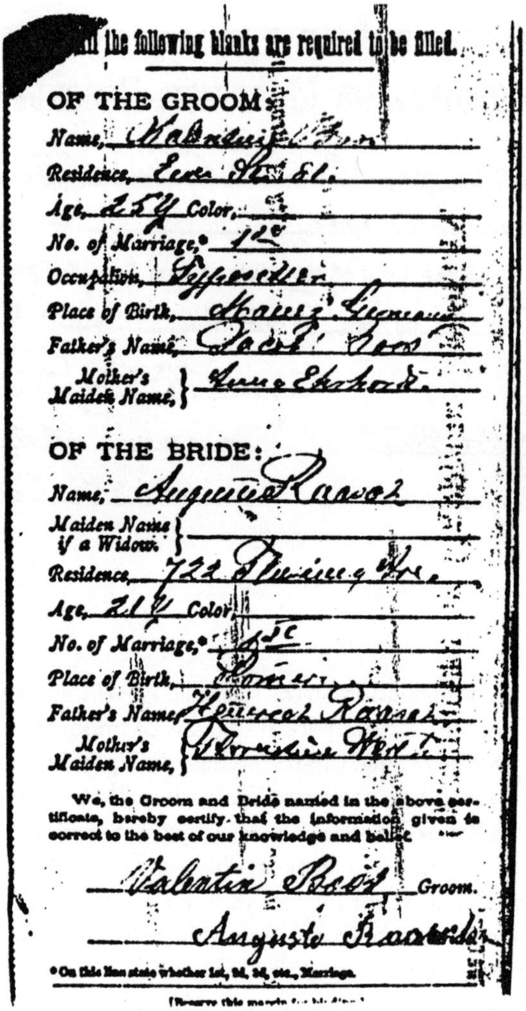

... the following blanks are required to be filled.

OF THE GROOM:

Name,

Residence,

Age, 25 Y Color,

No. of Marriage,* 1st

Occupation,

Place of Birth,

Father's Name,

Mother's Maiden Name,

OF THE BRIDE:

Name,

Maiden Name if a Widow,

Residence, 722

Age, 21 Y Color,

No. of Marriage,* 1st

Place of Birth,

Father's Name,

Mother's Maiden Name,

We, the Groom and Bride named in the above certificate, hereby certify that the information given is correct to the best of our knowledge and belief.

Valentin Boos, Groom.

Auguste

*On this line state whether 1st, 2d, 3d, etc., Marriage.

Illustration 2.3

Lastly, the signatures. Valentine Boos writes with an elegant hand, dropping the final "e" that the Americans had given his first name. Augusta uses the German spelling of her first name also—"Auguste." Her writing is smaller, but clear. Obviously, both could read and write, and possibly still spoke primarily German, as they clung to the German spellings of their names.

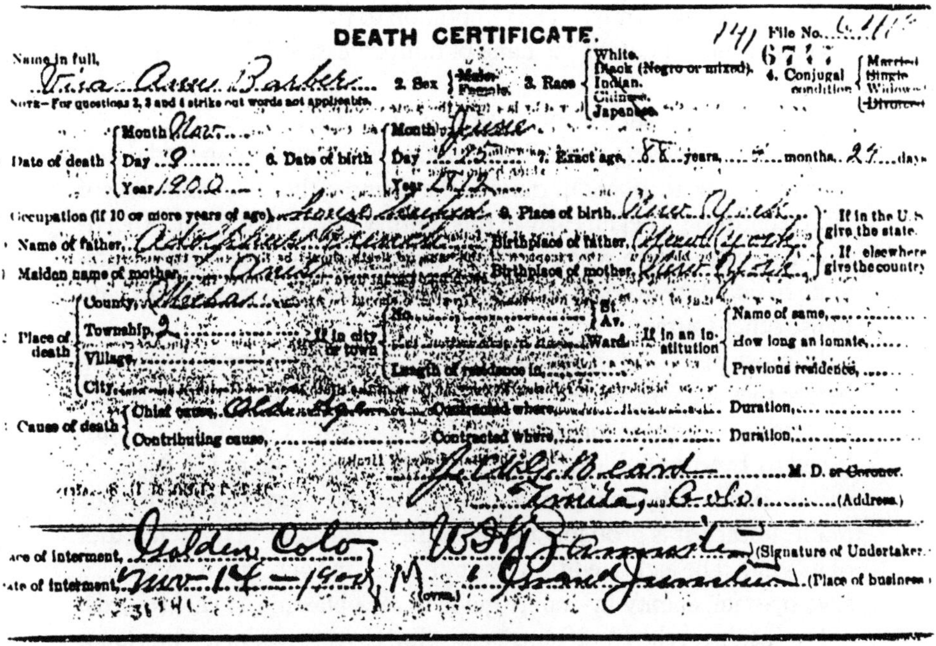
DEATH CERTIFICATE.

File No. 6717

Name in full, Vira Ann Barber 2. Sex Male Female 3. Race White. Black (Negro or mixed). Indian. Chinese. Japanese. 4. Conjugal condition Married Single Widowed Divorced

NOTE—For questions 2, 3 and 4 strike out words not applicable.

Date of death Month Nov Day 9 Year 1900 6. Date of birth Month June Day 25 Year 1812 7. Exact age 88 years 5 months 24 days

Occupation (if 10 or more years of age) House keeper 8. Place of birth New York

Name of father, Adolphus French Birthplace of father, New York

Maiden name of mother, Annis Birthplace of mother, New York

If in the U. S. give the state. If elsewhere give the country.

Place of death County, Otero Township, 2 Village, City, If in city or town No. St. Av. Ward. Length of residence in If in an institution Name of same, How long an inmate, Previous residence,

Cause of death Chief cause, Old Age Contracted where Duration, Contributing cause, Contracted where, Duration,

J. W. G. Beard M. D. or Coroner. Trinidad, Colo (Address.)

Place of interment, Golden Colo W. B. Hannister (Signature of Undertaker.)

Date of interment, Nov 14 – 1900 Grand Junction (Place of business.)

Illustration 2.4

Not bad. From the evidence, I deduce that my great-grandparents were proud of their heritage, well educated, and off to a promising start in the New World. I begin to hear their voices.

Illustration 2.4 shows the death record of my third great-grandmother, Vira Ann Barber. It gives her exact date of birth, date and residence at death, place of birth, and cause of death. It also states that she was a widow, buried in Golden, Colorado, on November 14, 1900. From this document, I gleaned the all-important link back one more generation. It was my first acquaintance with her parents.

There is a story with a moral attached here. Before sending for this certificate, I had done a lot of fruitless speculation on Vira Ann's parentage, even making the mistake of assuming someone else was her father because he lived in the same county at the time of her marriage. Finally, on the slim chance that her death would be recorded (many or most were not at this early date in Colorado history), I sent for this certificate. I found that her parents were two people I had never heard of before, Adolphus and Annis French! Holmes would have rebuked me firmly: "The temptation to form premature theories upon insufficient data is the bane of our profession." I hope I learned my lesson.

As you can see, such records are a family historian's gold mine if you can get your hands on them. They contain much more than bald dates. Unfortunately, throughout most of the country, the state-recording of vital records only began early in this century or late in the last. Appendix A gives the date when official record-keeping began on a statewide basis. Once you get back beyond that time period, you will have to use other sources.

In most places, vital records were kept on the county level long before they were recorded by the state. An almost indispensable tool for finding county records is *The Handybook for Genealogists*, published by Everton Publishers, Inc., P.O. Box 368, Logan, UT 84321. It can be ordered by mail, or found in the genealogy section of your public library. It is probably the most-used genealogical reference tool of its kind. The eighth edition was published in 1991, and it contains a state-by-state, county-by-county guide to the obtaining of vital records.

For instance, the *Handybook* entry for Calvert County, Maryland, gives the following information:

"Calvert County. Created 1654. Original County (formerly Patuxent). Address: Calvert County, 175 Main St., Prince Frederick, MD 20678-9302. Telephone: (301) 535-1600. Clerk of the Circuit Court has marriage records, divorce records, civil court records, land records, from 1882; Registrar of Wills has probate records from 1882; Courthouse burned 1882, most records destroyed; earlier records available from State Hall of Records."

In this record-gathering phase of your search, keep your eye out for obituaries. They are one of the richest sources there is. Typically they contain birth date and place, marriage date and place, parents' names, surviving siblings and descendants, and cemetery information, as well as biographical material that will flesh out the dates and give a voice to the dead. (Remember to maintain a healthy skepticism, however. Obituaries are written by survivors who may wish to play up or play down certain facts. Often the gaps are more significant than the substance.)

The basic rule of thumb in genealogy is to "leave no stone unturned." You are building a chain of evidence. The more information you can gather on each ancestor, the greater number of clues you will have to proceed with. On another level, the more you learn about them, the more you learn about yourself.

Once you have completed this initial phase of your detective work, a picture will start to form. Undoubtedly, you have collected many stories and begun to piece together a history, not out of history books, but out of the personal experiences of those who have lived, loved, and died in a time that is past. You have begun to hear their voices.

THREE

Constructing a Bridge

Even memory is not necessary for love. There is a land of the
living and a land of the dead and the bridge is love, the only
survival, the only meaning.
   —Thornton Wilder, *The Bridge of San Luis Rey*

How do you plan to chronicle the building of your bridge?

Your motives for researching your family history are key here. Perhaps you wish to do a traditional genealogy for yourself or your family, with a pedigree and family group sheets. Maybe you would like to concentrate on one particular line, your surname line for instance, take it back as far as you can, and then begin seeking descendants. Is your goal to gather all your living relations and have a vast "homecoming" reunion as Dorothy Spruill Redford did at the Somerset plantation? Or would you like to write a history of your family, or of one particular individual? Perhaps you are more interested in defining your genealogical identity than in tracing your family back to Charlemagne.

People do genealogy for many reasons, and seek different payoffs for their work. Your plan of action should be tailor-made for the payoff you expect to gain. This book suggests certain procedures that will facilitate your work, but what you do with the results is up to you. In my own experience, family history grows in meaning when it is shared. It is not really reasonable to expect your relatives to be excited about a pedigree chart with names and dates. In order for them to perceive and share your passion, you must share your insights. How can you best do this?

During the research process, as you gather details about your ancestors, you may want to consider keeping a record separate from the actual research facts, a sort of diary of your search and what it means to you. Using a spiral notebook, or a more formal type of journal, you might write about the people you find. Heading the page with a name, write how you feel about one of your recently found kin. What sense do you get of his/her life? Write your thoughts—free-form. The following is a short passage I wrote about how I perceive my great-grandmother, Augusta Raasch:

> Daughter of Prussia at the height of its power, you came to Brooklyn young. I can see you, slender and proud, your chin tilted high as you look down your long nose at the rabble of Lynch Street. This foreign, dirty street is not home. Home is gentle, green Pomerania where Grandmama still sits in her parlor sipping tea from the Polenska porcelain.
>
> You hold tightly to your identity, never intending to forget that you are descended from people of consequence. You must keep to the old ways, especially in this new place. Everything must be done the way Grandmama would have done it—perfectly and without apparent effort. Of course, Grandmama had servants, but even so, you must not give in to this new world, must not bend to its standards. If you bend, you will break, as Emily, your sister, did.

In connection with this, you might wish to write about what this person's life teaches you about yourself. Have you been influenced behaviorally, genetically, or materially by him/her? What insight into the human condition can you draw from looking at his/her life as a whole? My thoughts on Augusta continue in the following paragraphs:

> Though I never met you, Grandma Augusta, you have been a definite presence in my life. From you I inherited both my nose and my Polish passion. In you, that passion was sublimated into obsessive care for your home and family. Your perfectionism, zest for order, and devotion to tradition were passed on to your daughter, my grandmother, and those behaviors were bred into my own consciousness at an early age. But our times are different than yours. The world has changed, becoming infinitely more complex. Under your strong, uncomplicated value system, Prussia rose to great heights, only to be brought low because tyrants carried such ideas to extremes.
>
> Today I find your expectations a burden that I have had to deal with on my own terms. My house is orderly, most of the time, but I have had to throw out the perfectionism and unquestioning obe-

dience. I find that I do share your love of tradition, however, as a quality that can add substance and perspective to life. Your traditions are some of the many that color and give shape to my world, and they will be handed down to your great-great-grandchildren. Though modified by my own experience, your voice is still heard.

Such a record can later be used as a starting point for a more formal biography, but in the meantime, it can be a companion to your search, giving meaning to the names on the charts. For you will have to have charts. You will have to bring some order out of the chaos you are creating with your research. The bridge you are building, linking yourself to your kindred dead, must be a sound one, constructed according to plan, with each plank secured and each nail driven home.

Creating Your Own Blueprint

How do you begin this task? Different personality types solve the problem of organization in different ways. Sherlock Holmes was intuitive, right-brained, and notoriously untidy, but he was always able to lay his hand on what he wanted. Hercule Poirot was left-brained and a legend of order. Of course he had the invaluable Miss Lemon to keep his filing up to date.

As you undertake the problem of organizing your data, you need to develop a working system that will best suit both your personality and time-management requirements.

First of all, how much time do you have to devote to genealogy? If time is not a problem, you can undertake the most detailed research and file it and cross-file it elaborately. If, however, time is scarce, you will seriously want to consider using a computer. There are genealogy software programs available for every level of computer expertise. Those for novices are extremely user-friendly. I speak from experience. One of the first computerized tasks I undertook was genealogy. A review of several software programs is given in Appendix B.

Secondly, are you a Holmes or a Poirot? Do you find a minimum of organization all you require, or do you need something more detailed in order to work effectively? There are as many genealogical methods as there are genealogists. The important thing is to employ the method that will best facilitate your research. Don't become bogged down by detail. The longer you work, the more individualistic your method will become. Below are several different strategies. You might choose one of them to get started.

The place to start your organization is with your pedigree. Pedigree forms can be obtained in various ways. By far the best way is to buy one of the software packages reviewed in Appendix B. These programs generate all their own charts and forms, organizing and linking your data automatically, and making it possible to sort through it quickly. With a computer, you need record each individual only once. If you choose to do your records by hand or with a typewriter, you will have to enter each individual and his/her vital statistics three times—once on the pedigree chart, once on a family group sheet as a child, and once on a family group as a parent. If you decide to do your records by hand, however, consult Appendix C for a list of places where you might obtain forms.

Illustration 3.1 shows a computer-generated pedigree, made by using Personal Ancestral File, the most-popular and least-expensive genealogy software available.

Whatever forms you use, pedigrees are filled out in a standard way. You begin with yourself. The father's line is always at the top, the mother's line at the bottom. For genealogical purposes, women are always designated by their maiden name. Most forms have room for four generations. When you get past the first four, you begin new pedigree charts, starting with the last generation on Chart No. 1. Using Illustration 3.1 as an example, the first person on my Chart No. 2 will be Walter McGill Gibson. Chart No. 2 will show his pedigree back four more generations. Chart No. 3 will begin with Walter's wife, Mary Alice Campbell, Chart No. 4 with Valentine Sebastian Boos, and so on.

In addition to a pedigree chart, you will also need to make a family group sheet for each family on your pedigree, as shown in Illustration 3.2. If the husband or wife was married more than once, a separate sheet is needed for the second marriage, showing any children by that marriage. Illustration 3.3 shows the documentation, or source of information, for each person on the group sheet. *Maintaining records of sources is vital.* Sometimes you will come across conflicting dates or places, particularly as you begin to share data with other relatives. It is important to be able to identify the source of your information so that you may determine which is the more accurate.

PEDIGREE CHART

7 Sep 1992

Chart no. 1

```
                                                                    8 Walter McGill GIBSON-9-------------------
                                                                      BORN:    9 Feb 1845
                                                                      PLACE: Northville,Wayne,Michigan
                                                                      MARR:   28 Oct 1886   --3
                                            4 Nathan Alexander GIBSON-6----------------   PLACE: East Saginaw,Saginaw,Michigan
                                              BORN:    5 Oct 1889                         DIED:    1 Apr 1913
                                              PLACE: Saginaw,Saginaw,Michigan             PLACE: Detroit,Wayne,Michigan
                                              MARR:    3 Jul 1916   --2
                                              PLACE: Detroit,Wayne,Michigan             9 Mary Alice CAMPBELL-10-------------------
                                              DIED:   14 Mar 1962                         BORN:   14 May 1862
                                              PLACE: Arcadia,LA,California                PLACE: Southwold,Elgin,O,Canada
                                                                                         DIED:    1 Apr 1929
               2 Robert Valentine GIBSON-1----------------                               PLACE: Detroit,Wayne,Michigan
                 BORN:    7 Feb 1921
                 PLACE: Indianapolis,Marion,Indiana                                   10 Valentine Sebastian BOOS-22--------------
                 MARR:   12 Oct 1944   --1                                               BORN:   12 Jul 1858
                 PLACE: Raymond,Pacific,Washington                                       PLACE: Mainz,Rheinhessen,Germany
                 DIED:                                                                   MARR:   17 Feb 1883   --5
                 PLACE:                                                                  PLACE: Brooklyn,Kings,New York
                                            5 Emily Pauline BOOS-7--------------------   DIED:   18 Feb 1924
                                              BORN:   25 Sep 1888                         PLACE: Saginaw,Saginaw,Michigan
                                              PLACE: Hamden,New Haven,Connecticut
                                              DIED:   25 Feb 1978                      11 Ida Augusta Emilie RAASCH-23-------------
                                              PLACE: Newport Beach,O,California           BORN:   27 Aug 1861
               1 Gail Valerie GIBSON-3--------------------                                PLACE: Ratzebuhr,Pommern,P,Germany
                 BORN:   24 Jul 1947                                                     DIED:   10 Apr 1920
                 PLACE: Fresno,Fresno,California                                         PLACE: Saginaw,Saginaw,Michigan
                 MARR:   21 Oct 1972   --97
                 PLACE: Arcadia,LA,California                                          12 Heinrich HENKEL-177-------------------
                 DIED:                                                                   BORN:   23 Jan 1876
                 PLACE:                                                                   PLACE: Doerhof,Russia
               David Peter VANDAGRIFF-422-----------                                     MARR:   Abt    1896    --39
                 Spouse                                                                   PLACE: Doerhof,,Russia
                                                                                         DIED:   20 Jul 1955
                                            6 Henry HENKEL-176------------------------   PLACE: Portland,Multnomah,Oregon
                                              BORN:   20 Mar 1897
                                              PLACE: Doerhof,Russia                    13 Katherine LOHRENGEL-178-----------------
                                              MARR:   22 May 1922   --38                  BORN:         1880
                                              PLACE: South Bend,,Washington               PLACE: Doerhof,Russia
                                              DIED:    1 Apr 1972                         BUR.:   13 Jan 1915
                                              PLACE: Tuscon,Pima,Arizona                  PLACE: Tacoma,Pierce,Washington
               3 Maxine Catherine HENKLE-2----------------
                 BORN:   25 Jan 1923                                                   14 Melvin Martin BARBER-193-----------------
                 PLACE: Raymond,Pacific,Washington                                       BORN:   11 Sep 1873
                 DIED:                                                                    PLACE: Hampton,Rock Island,Illinois
                 PLACE:                                                                   MARR:   24 Jun 1897(div)   --43
                                            7 Roxie Hannah BARBER-175-----------------   PLACE: Redmond,Sevier,Utah
                                              BORN:   24 Oct 1902                         DIED:   18 Feb 1951
                                              PLACE: Redmond,Sevier,Utah                  PLACE: Raymond,Pacific,Washington
               Name and address of submitter:  DIED:
                                              PLACE:                                   15 Johannah Brighamina POULSON-426----------
                                                                                         BORN:    5 Oct 1877
                                                                                         PLACE: Redmond,Sevier,Utah
                                                                                         DIED:   23 Apr 1950
               Phone:                                                                    PLACE: Raymond,Pacific,Washington
```

Illustration 3.1

Now we have come to the place where you must choose your individual method. What are you going to do with the evidence—with certificates, notes, and other documentation you have acquired for each name on your pedigree?

To begin with, a good idea is to buy a portable file box, label the tabs with each surname on your pedigree, and file the information as you get it. Spend your time in the beginning researching, not setting up an elaborate filing system.

Later on, as your evidence accumulates, you will want to consider a more permanent solution. My method is somewhat Holmesian, com-

```
                              FAMILY GROUP RECORD-3
  7 Sep 1992                                                        Page 1   of 2
  =================================================================================
  HUSBAND Walter McGill GIBSON-9
  ---------------------------------------------------------------------------------
  BORN:     9 Feb 1845        PLACE: Northville,Wayne,Michigan
  CHR.:                       PLACE:
  DIED:     1 Apr 1913        PLACE: Detroit,Wayne,Michigan
  BUR.:                       PLACE: Oakwood Cemetery,Bridgeport,Saginaw,Michigan
  MARR:    28 Oct 1886        PLACE: East Saginaw,Saginaw,Michigan
  FATHER: Nathaniel GIBSON-11                                   PARENTS' MRIN: 4
  MOTHER: Bridget MCGILL-12
  =================================================================================
  WIFE    Mary Alice CAMPBELL-10
  ---------------------------------------------------------------------------------
  BORN:    14 May 1862        PLACE: Southwold,Elgin,Ontario,Canada
  CHR.:                       PLACE:
  DIED:     1 Apr 1929        PLACE: Detroit,Wayne,Michigan
  BUR.:                       PLACE:
  FATHER: Alexander McIntosh CAMPBELL-41                        PARENTS' MRIN: 12
  MOTHER: Lucretia SAUNDERS-42
  =================================================================================
  CHILDREN
  =================================================================================
  1.  NAME: Nathan Alexander GIBSON-6
  ---- BORN: 5 Oct 1889       PLACE: Saginaw,Saginaw,Michigan
  M    CHR.:                  PLACE:
       DIED: 14 Mar 1962      PLACE: Arcadia,Los Angeles,California
       BUR.:                  PLACE: Monrovia,Los Angeles,California
       SPOUSE: Emily Pauline BOOS-7                             MRIN: 2
       MARR: 3 Jul 1916       PLACE: Detroit,Wayne,Michigan
  ---------------------------------------------------------------------------------
  2.  NAME:
  ---- BORN:                  PLACE:
       CHR.:                  PLACE:
       DIED:                  PLACE:
       BUR.:                  PLACE:
       SPOUSE:
       MARR:                  PLACE:
  ---------------------------------------------------------------------------------
  3.  NAME:
  ---- BORN:                  PLACE:
       CHR.:                  PLACE:
       DIED:                  PLACE:
       BUR.:                  PLACE:
       SPOUSE:
       MARR:                  PLACE:
  ---------------------------------------------------------------------------------
  4.  NAME:
  ---- BORN:                  PLACE:
       CHR.:                  PLACE:
       DIED:                  PLACE:
       BUR.:                  PLACE:
       SPOUSE:
       MARR:                  PLACE:
  =================================================================================
```

Illustration 3.2

bining several different techniques. In my permanent filing cabinet, I keep a file on each surname that contains the originals of all my documents as well as data I am not currently using. This includes everything that I have used to assemble my pedigree as it stands today.

My pedigree, which is now over two hundred pages long, is kept in a permanent loose-leaf notebook. I don't carry it around with me, because I don't need it. I have never printed out all of my family group sheets. To do so would take hours, as I now have literally hundreds of families. Instead, I keep them safe on the hard drive of my computer, with current backups in my disk drawer and in my safety deposit box.

```
                          FAMILY GROUP RECORD-3
                             DOCUMENTATION

7 Sep 1992                                                        Page 2  of 2
============================================================================
HUSBAND     Walter McGill GIBSON-9                               Yr of Birth 1845
WIFE        Mary Alice CAMPBELL-10                               Yr of Birth 1862
----------------------------------------------------------------------------

HUSBAND  - Walter McGill GIBSON-9
           Source: McGill Family Bible, Marriage Certificate by correspondence, obituary
           printed in the Saginaw Courier-Herald.

WIFE     - Mary Alice CAMPBELL-10
           Death Certificate by correspondence, gave birth and death information.
           Parents names obtained from Bruce Campbell, Jr., 3rd cousin.  Verified in 1880
           census of Saginaw, Michigan.

CHILD  1 - Nathan Alexander GIBSON-6
           Birth recorded in McGill Family Bible.  Verified by death certificate.
           Marriage information taken from marriage certificate in possession of widow
============================================================================
```

Illustration 3.3

For current research, I keep notebooks on the surnames I am working on. These notebooks contain all the information I have on my end
of the line for an individual with that surname, with a separate section
for his or her descendants and their information. In the notebooks I
keep pertinent family group sheets, copies of documents, letters, and
obituaries, and biographical sheets. This prevents having to search
through stacks of papers to find the document "I know I have somewhere." If I am going to do research on a particular family, I just grab
the appropriate notebook and I'm ready to go.

Maintaining these notebooks is painless. All you need is a three-
hole punch and a three-ring binder. It is also satisfying. As you organize your materials, it is surprising what ideas will leap to mind. You
will, simply by putting places and dates together, arrive at key insights
into the lives of your ancestors. Obvious gaps will appear, indicating
that more investigation is necessary. New paths of inquiry will occur
to you. But take heed! Genealogy is habit-forming! The more information you find, the more intrigued you become, and the more you
will want to find.

If you are meticulous by nature and have the time to invest in careful organization, I recommend *Managing a Genealogical Project*, by
William Dollarhide, published by the Genealogical Publishing Company, Inc., Baltimore, Maryland. Dollarhide is also the creator of
Everyone's Family Tree, a genealogical software product that I review
in Appendix B. His book offers excellent advice for the dedicated
genealogist who is managing a large amount of data. Several different
filing and numbering systems are introduced. He also discusses creat-

ing your own data base for storing and collating information, and creating research journals and logs, and includes a selection of master forms. To order this book, or any of the standard charts and forms, telephone the Dollarhide Systems at 1-800-733-3807. They are extremely helpful and friendly.

One very useful hint I picked up from Dollarhide is to staple all scraps of information onto standard-size notebook paper so that nothing will be lost. He then suggests numbering each page of the notebook, so that you need only refer to the notebook and page number as your source of information on group sheets or family histories.

Doing an Evaluation

The purpose of whatever filing system you decide to use should be to compose your data clearly, in a way that will enable you to see where you need to go. Once you have brought some semblance of order to your research and entered everything you have on your pedigree and family groups, take a look at the earliest individuals on each of your family lines. How much do you know about them?

Illustration 3.4 shows a sample biographical sheet on Adolphus French, my fourth great-grandfather. The only information I had at this time came from: (1) The death certificate of my third great-grandmother, Vira Ann French, shown in Chapter Two (name of parents and her date and place of birth); (2) Vira Ann French's marriage record in Kalamazoo, Michigan, and those of her two sisters and brother; (3) The family group information gleaned from the laundry ledger mentioned in Chapter Two that my cousin's grandmother kept during the Civil War. (Now you can see why it was so important!)

All the original notes and certificates concerning Adolphus are in my notebook, but I needed to distill them into this chronological summary in order to have a better grasp of the situation. Adolphus French was a man, not a bunch of certificates. Making a biographical sheet of his life helps me to see him as a real person, stimulates questions in my mind, and inspires possible courses of action.

Now it's your turn. Get out all your clues for each end-of-the-line individual and sift your evidence carefully. Then write out your biographical sheets, organizing them chronologically as though each one were a time line. Where are the gaps? What do you need to know in order to find this person's parents? Have you obtained everything you

ADOLPHUS FRENCH

1783: born on 8 Dec in Mass.
1805 (circa): married Annis Grinnell in Mass? Both born Mass.
1806: Birth of Almira French.
1807: Birth of Adolphus French.
1808: Birth of Ethan French.
1810: Birth of Laura French.
1812: Birth of Permelia French.
1813: Birth of Vira Ann French in N.Y.
1816: Birth of Cordelia French.
1817: Birth of Enos French.
1818: Birth of Wealthy French in N.Y.
1820: Birth of Mary French.
1822: Birth of Sophia French.
1824: Birth of Louisa H. French in N.Y.
1825: Birth of Lorenzo French.
1827: Birth of Judson French.
1828: Death of Judson French.
1830: Birth of Amanda French.
1831: Death of Lorenzo French (Feb), Laura
      French (Aug), and wife Annis (Dec).
1833: Marriage of Ethan French Jan 1 in Kalamazoo, Mich.
1834: Marriage of daughter Permelia, Kalamazoo, Mich., 2 Oct.
1835: Marriage of daughter Vira Ann, Kalamazoo, Mich., 1 Nov.
      Death of Permelia French Vickery on 18 Nov.
1836: Marriage of daughter Wealthy, Kalamazoo, 14 Oct.
1840: Vira Ann and Jonas Barber living in Princeton, Scott, Iowa.
1843: Marriage of daughter Louisa, in Rock Island, Ill.
1847: Death of Ethan French (Jan).
1850: Death of Adolphus on 27 Apr.

QUESTIONS:
1. Where did Adolphus come from in Massachusetts
2. Who were his parents?
3. Where did he live in New York?
4. What happened to all of his children?
5. Did Adolphus accompany Vira Ann, Wealthy, Permelia, and Ethan
    to Kalamazoo after the death of Annis?
6. Where did Annis and Adolphus die?

ACTION:

1. Write Mary Herr at Scott County Library to try to get
    death record for Adolphus and marriages for Adolphus's
    other children.
2. Do Census search on Adolphus.
3. Track descendants of Adolphus to find more info on him.

Illustration 3.4

can from living relatives, vital records? What sense do you get about this ancestor? What were his interests? Can you begin to detect a voice behind the dates and places?

After you have accomplished this task, you should have a clearer idea of where you need to go and what you need to do. Set a research goal or goals for that person. My goal is to answer the questions at the bottom of Adolphus's sheet. By brainstorming, I came up with three action steps. When I have answered all my questions, I will have completed my research goal. Then I will begin biographical sheets for Adolphus's parents, following the same procedure.

What are your goals? List them. Under action steps, list any ideas you may have. In the following chapters you will find additional ways you can add to your store of information and reach your goals.

What's Important and What's Not?

You are a detective. Your clues are vital. Whatever filing system you use, be sure to preserve all your reference documents, even if you don't see how they can possibly fit into the picture.

If there is a cardinal rule in genealogy, it is *don't throw anything away*! Sometimes we can only build our bridge with toothpicks. Each one is a mere scrap of information, an impression. Put together, however, they eventually create a solid plank.

Remember that you are looking for people, not just names and dates. People's possessions often contain clues to their personalities as well as their identity. One of the items I treasure most will never fit in a file box. It is a small, battered cardboard suitcase measuring 12″ ×9″ ×4″. This suitcase sits incongruously amidst the French Provincial furniture of my bedroom, scarred, stuck all over with peeling ship labels, and tied with a nearly indecipherable tag reading "Mother's and Widow's Pilgrimage, Destination: Hotel McAlpin, N.Y., N.Y." My great-grandmother took this tiny suitcase with her when she went with the "Gold Star Mothers" to see her oldest son's grave in France. He was killed in the Argonne Forest in World War I at the age of nineteen.

But before that sad journey, the suitcase served another purpose. It actually belonged to her son-in-law, my grandfather. The tiny receptacle and its contents were all that my grandfather possessed when he left home at age fifteen, following the death of his mother. The son of German-Russian immigrants, he didn't have a lot of possessions, but in his suitcase he kept his treasures. The oldest—a 1910 edition of the *Morning Oregonian* sports page—still remains carefully folded on the bottom.

Starting with that pitifully small suitcase, my grandfather launched himself into what was to become a successful, happy life. From modest beginnings as a baker's assistant, he excelled at several professions, finally finding his true niche in his fifties when he became a real estate developer in Southern California. Whenever I look at that suitcase, I remember my grandfather. First I see a sad young man leaving home in tears. Then I remember the man I knew—his practical jokes, his cigar, his Groucho Marx lift of the eyebrows.

To me, the suitcase will always be a reminder that a life that started out with so much sorrow and such little promise was transformed by fortitude and determination. That suitcase is what family history is all about. Its owner's stubborn determination is one of the dominant voices in my own blood.

FOUR

Starting to Build

The art of building . . . is the beginning of all the arts that lie
outside the person.

—Havelock Ellis, *The Dance of Life*

You have gathered all the evidence you can from living relatives, you
have confirmed it, you have organized and sifted it. You have collated
your facts into biographical sheets for each end-of-the-line individual,
or each person you need to know more about. Now it is time to start
to build on the foundation of what you have.

This is where family history gets exciting. You are about to uncover
facts that go back beyond anyone's living memory. You will discover
perhaps why Great-aunt Sophia has such domineering ways, why one
line of your family is riddled with divorces, why another line produces
people of hope and fortitude.

While we certainly can't blame everything on our heritage, there
are definite strains that seem to run through families—dysfunction,
faith, achievement, failure.

My father has always been motivated by a vision that sees beyond present events. He has never been afraid of change. These are qualities that
I believe were sown in him according to the "traditions of his fathers."

His Grandfather Boos found life with his own father, a newspaper
editor in Mainz, Germany, too confining, too restrictive. He was not
afraid to sail for America at an early age and pursue his trade from the
ground up in a foreign country. Beginning as a typesetter, he died the
successful editor of his own newspaper. What is interesting, however,
is that he in his turn became a confining, restrictive father! Because my
grandmother was the youngest daughter, he expected her to stay home
and care for her parents instead of marrying. This would have been
her role, had she been raised in Germany. However, my grandmother

had enough of her father's spirit not to settle for such a fate. In a year (1914) when women were not particularly employable, she ran away from Saginaw, Michigan, to the big city of Detroit, where she found a job as a secretary. Not too many years later, she eloped with my grandfather, and became, in time, a strict parent herself.

My father's home life was tempered by the nature of his father, luckily, and what had been the negative Boos characteristic of control and domination was watered down, leaving him with the positive attributes of courage and vision.

Often in our search, we will find evidence that surprises and delights us. My husband, the grandson of a Methodist minister, has donated hours of his time serving as a lay leader in our church. As we did his genealogy, we found that he was descended from a long line of ministers, beginning with several who escaped to New England from their mother country in order to avoid a death sentence for preaching a nonconformist religion. All in all, there were nineteen ministers in his direct line, most of whom preached stirring sermons at one time or another in the Old North Church in Boston. Religious oratory and conviction would seem to be in his blood.

Choose a line that particularly interests you. Perhaps you wish to trace a particular dysfunction, solve a mystery, or find out if an old family legend is based in fact. Now is the time to focus your energy and ingenuity on your goal and press forward!

Obtaining County Records by Correspondence

In Chapter Two it was mentioned that many county records have been kept for a longer period of time than state records. In New England you will find an even better situation. Each town kept records, which, if they still exist, give births, deaths, marriages, and a variety of other information, such as when a particular individual moved away and why. Some towns in the Midwest kept similar early records.

Everton's *Handybook for Genealogists* lists each county, and tells what records are available by correspondence and where to write. Writing for records is almost as good as a visit to the county, and should certainly be considered before making a costly trip. Typically, the available records would be the following: birth, death, marriage, divorce, probate, and land records. The first four are fairly obvious, but what information can be gleaned from land records? You might be surprised.

Illustration 4.1 shows a copy of a page in the Saginaw County Deed Book. The first entry shows that a Mr. Paine and his wife sold a parcel of land to my second great-grandmother, Bridget (McGill) Gibson, for $913.00. This tells me that Bridget must have come into a substantial sum of money in February of 1864. Did a relative die and leave it to her? How else would she have come by such a great sum in those days on the edge of the frontier? This is possibly a clue to the death date of her father or mother. She buys the property in her own name, which also tells me something about her, namely that she knew property was a good investment (later records show that when the land finally passed out of the family in 1883 it was sold for $2,500.00), and she was a woman capable of making and executing decisions in an era when most women left such decisions to their husbands.

Entry eight on the same page is actually a will, where she bequeaths the property she had bought to her husband, Nathaniel Gibson, whom she also names as sole executor of her estate. Nathaniel later leaves it to his son, my great-grandfather, Walter McGill Gibson, who conveys it to his first wife, Mary T. Gibson. Thus through the land records I can confirm or trace relationships: Bridget was the wife of Nathaniel Gibson; Walter was the son of Bridget and Nathaniel; Walter was married to Mary T. Gibson in 1882.

Land records may contain the only proof of relationship you will ever find. In most places, land records precede the keeping of probate records. Also, before 1850, wives' names are *not* listed on the census, but they *are* given on the land records.

Even though early deeds are difficult to read, it is important that you attempt to read them in their entirety. They may contain surprises in the midst of all the legal language. As I proceeded with my inquiry on Adolphus French, my fourth great-grandfather, I found out through the 1810 and 1820 Census Index (more on censuses in Chapter Five), that he lived in Spafford, Onondaga County, New York, during those years. Illustration 4.2 shows a copy of a grantor (seller) deed index for Onondaga County, New York. Near the bottom you can see that my ancestor Adolphus French and his wife Annis appear to have sold land to J. B. Eggleston in 1827. A grantee index had previously shown the purchase of the same Lot 21 in 1816. From the indexes, the transaction appears cut-and-dried.

Upon ordering the deeds themselves, however, a different story

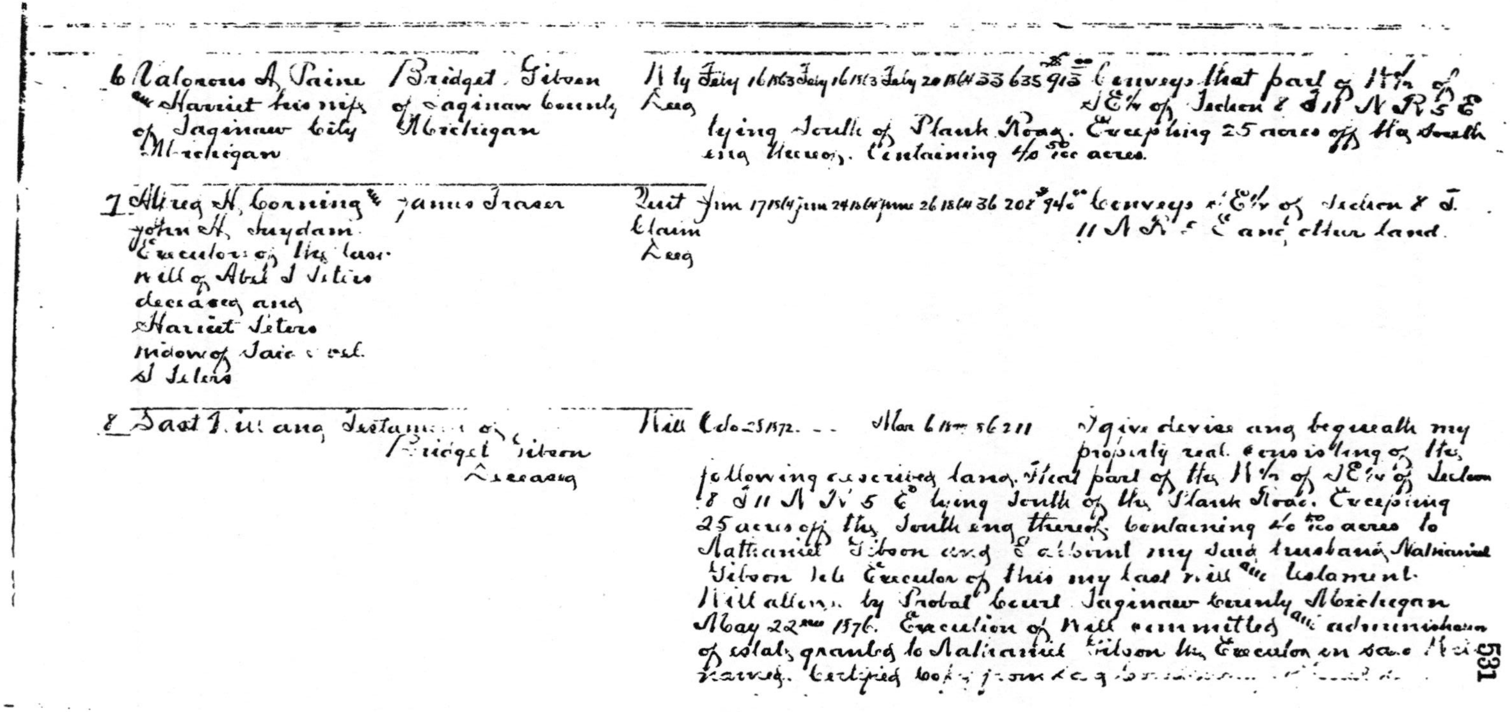

6	Valorous A. Paine and Harriet his wife of Saginaw City Michigan	Bridget Gibson of Saginaw County Michigan	W ty Deed	Feby 16 1863	Feby 16 1863	Feby 20 1864	33	635	$915 — Conveys that part of N½ of SE¼ of Section 8 T 11 N R 5 E lying South of Plank Road. Excepting 25 acres off the South end thereof. Containing 40/100 acres.
7	Alfred H. Corning and John H. Suydam Executors of the last will of Abel S. Peters deceased and Harriet Peters widow of said Abel S. Peters	James Fraser	Quit Claim Deed	Jun 17 1864	Jun 24 1864	June 26 1864	36	202	$940 — Conveys [illegible] E½ of Section 8 T. 11 N R 5 E and other land.
8	Last Will and Testament of Bridget Gibson Deceased		Will	Octo 25 1872		Mar 6 1879	56	211	I give devise and bequeath my property real consisting of the following described land. That part of the N½ of SE¼ of Section 8 T 11 N R 5 E lying South of the Plank Road. Excepting 25 acres off the South end thereof containing 40/100 acres to Nathaniel Gibson and [illegible] my said husband Nathaniel Gibson sole Executor of this my last will and testament. Will allowed by Probate Court Saginaw County Michigan May 22nd 1876. Execution of Will committed and administration of estate granted to Nathaniel Gibson the Executor in said Will named. Certified copy [illegible]

Illustration 4.1

INDEX TO DEEDS - GRANTORS - ONONDAGA COUNTY, N. Y., FROM 1794 TO 1870.

YEAR	A...E F G H	I...O	K L M N O P Q	Q R S T U V W X Y Z	CRANTOR	GRANTEE	BOOK	PAGE	LOCL	LOT	BLOCK	TRACT
1795		Jacobus			Truer	A. Smith	1CR	366	Cic	7		
1796				Samuel	Truer	J. Atkinson	1CR	371	Tully	36		
"		Peter			Credenbagh	J. Hagerman	1CR	377	Cata	75		
1796	Abaham				Truer	A. C. Clmendorph	1CJ	75	Cic	4		
1795	Abaham				Truer	N. Fish	1CJ	276	Lya	47		
1795		John			Crederick	C. Childs	1CJ	413	Tully	41		
1794	Abaham				Truer	N. Fish	1CJ	512	Tim	70		
1795	Abaham				Truer	R. L. Hooper Jr	1CJ	37		L.		
"	Abaham				Truer	R. L. Hooper Jr	1CJ	70	Cic	72		
1801			Marritie Samuel		Truer	S. Ingals	B	125	Home	74		
1804			Milman		Trench	C. Puffer	C	447	Fab	92		
1805			Milman		Trench	J. Olcop	D	455	Fab	92		
1806		John			Crederick	J. Sloot	F	331	Tully	41		
1807			Martha		Trench							
"			Philemon		Trench	J. Crouch	G	243	Fab	92		
1811		Joseph			Treligh	C. C. White	L	205				
1815	Huldah			Smith	Treeman	M. McNair	Q	426	Ham	44		
1816	Charles		Loisa		Trench	J. B. Chapman	R	654	Man	7		
1816	Amasa				Treeman	J. K. Ladd	U	127	Fab	32		
1819			Cuther		Trench							
"			Lucy		Trench	R. Pomeroy	W	347	Cts	4		
1822	Ebenezer			Rachel	Trench	U. French & ano	AA	384	Otis	44		
"	Achbel	Hannah	Louisa	Sumner J	Trench	J. Lyman	AA	315	Otis	4		
1823	Anna				Treeman							
"	Charles				Treeman	J. Everson	CC	349	Man	69		
1826		John	Mary		Treeman et al	U. Phillips	JB	325	Sal	9		
"	Artemas				L. Treeman	W. Chatfield	HH	245	Man	22		
"	Benjamin	Ephraim	Marilla		Trench							
"	Betsey				Trench	J. Dunham et al	HH	430	Cic	73		
"	Benjamin		Marilla		Trench	C. Trench	HH	432	Cic	76		
1827	Adolphus				Trench							
"	Annis				Trench	R. B. Eggleston	JJ	393	Spaf	21		
"			Cuther		French by Ad	A. Betts	LL	313	Otis	99		
1828			Philemon		Trench	J. French et al	NN	101	Man	67		

Illustration 4.2

emerged. The purchase did take place in 1816. Adolphus purchased fifty-five-acre Lot 21 from Levi Foster for $570.00. However, the *sale recorded in 1827 actually took place in 1818.* A careful inspection of the deed also revealed that only thirty-nine acres of the entire fifty-five-acre lot were sold to Mr. Eggleston for a sum of $800.00. Why the discrepancy in dates? The actual sale of the land and the recording of the deed are two different transactions. The recording of the deed is the job of the purchaser and is his only proof of title. For some reason, J. B. Eggleston delayed recording his purchase, possibly doing so only when he was ready to sell the land himself.

For purposes of family history, what does the deed tell me that the index doesn't? First of all, it shows that Adolphus's land appreciated 71 percent in two years, and that he realized that appreciation. Further study of land values in the area show that in 1827 the same lot was worth only $550.00, so if he had waited until 1827 to sell, he would have lost money on the land. Also, the sale of thirty-nine of his fifty-five acres indicates that Adolphus had given up his attempt at crop-based agriculture, retaining only sixteen acres for himself and his family. Future events were to prove his decision to sell in 1818 a prudent one. By 1827 farmers in Onondaga were in a desperate situation, with cheap western wheat causing prices to plunge.

Land records will often tell where a family came from. When my third great-grandfather, Jonas Barber, bought property in Kalamazoo, the land records revealed that he had come from Pennsylvania. This was a vital clue, telling me what state to search for Jonas Barber's beginnings.

If you are not satisfied that your correspondents in the county courthouses have turned over every stone, you may wish to search these county records yourself. Many of them have been microfilmed and can be ordered through your local Family History Center at the Church of Jesus Christ of Latter-day Saints. Throughout this book, I will be referring to the Family History Centers, which offer you free access to the largest genealogy library in the world in Salt Lake City. Because of its strong beliefs about family, the LDS church places a very high priority on family history. These centers are a primary resource for the genealogist. Chapter Seven will give the details on how to order county records through your local Family History Center.

Searching indexes of death records can be particularly rewarding as they will give you a lead on obituaries not only for members of your direct line, but for their relatives as well.

Probate records can contain vital clues to family members. When researching my very prolific Heavlin line in Harrison County, Ohio,

I found that there were an enormous number of families with that name. Two brothers, Stephen and Samuel, had moved there at the end of the eighteenth century, married sisters, and proceeded enthusiastically to multiply. Stephen had left a will, fortunately, listing all of his ten children. Using the will, I was able to untangle the knot of children, grandchildren, and great-grandchildren, figuring out who belonged to which family.

Even if you know all the members of a family, probate records are still valuable. Wills used to be much more individually worded than they are today. In this final record, your ancestor may speak quite clearly. What did he want his family members to know after he died? How did he feel about each of them? What kind of an estate did he have to leave? What things did he consider to be of the most value?

When Jonas Barber died, he left his considerable wealth and all his business interests to his wife, though he had three living sons. This tells me that he respected her competence and wished her to have the dignity of an independent income. It speaks highly of their relationship in an era (he died in 1880) when women were not ordinarily concerned in business pursuits.

If records are not available through the Family History Center, and you wish to visit the courthouses in person, be certain to telephone first. While these records are technically in the public domain, some courthouses only give access to licensed genealogists. This is because most old records are in extremely fragile condition. I ran up against this problem in Northampton, Massachusetts, and got around it by hiring a librarian from the county library to examine the records and transcribe them by hand.

Corresponding with Libraries and Societies

Three excellent sources for libraries and historical and genealogical societies in the counties of the U.S. are: *Compendium of Historical Sources*, by Ronald A. Bremer; *The Source, A Guidebook of American Genealogy*, edited by John Cerny and Arlene Eakle; and the aforementioned *Handybook for Genealogists*, by Everton Publishers. All of these books will be available in any good library. From them you can glean the names and addresses of libraries and societies in the area where you are searching. These entities can be immensely helpful, as much of the information you need may already have been researched and indexed by them. A good librarian or society volunteer is worth her weight in gold.

Using my *Handybook*, I found the listing for the public library in Saginaw and wrote, requesting an obituary for my great-grandmother Augusta (Raasch) Boos. I got a lovely, prompt letter from an angel librarian named Peggy Lugthart who had managed to find what I wanted. The obituary (Illustration 4.3) proved to possess vital clues—my great-grandparents had been married in Brooklyn in 1883, and Augusta was born in Neustettin, Germany, immigrating from Prussia about 1871. With the marriage year and place, I was able to write to Brooklyn for marriage records. I received the certificate we examined in Chapter Two, which gave the name of her father and her mother's maiden name. This led, of course, to further discoveries I will detail later.

I have corresponded with Peggy Lugthart for five years. During that time she has dug up an incredible assortment of information that I could never have discovered on my own. My second great-grandfather, Nathaniel Gibson, had the first hardware store in Saginaw. She sent me advertisements and snippets about it from the county history. She unearthed his obituary, which was very old, printed in 1880. She sent me the above-mentioned page in the Saginaw County deed book. On her own initiative, Peggy tracked all of Nathaniel's descendants, sent me stories about them from the county history and newspapers, as well as cemetery records and obituaries. When she went to New York to do her own research, she found herself in the county where one of Nathaniel's daughters had gone to live after her marriage. Remembering this, she looked up land records for me. She even called me long distance to tell me what she had found! Obviously, this sort of bonding with your librarian doesn't happen often.

What kind of information can you request from libraries and societies?
1. Obituaries. You will need death date.
2. Cemetery records. For this you usually only need a name, or better a family group sheet. These records will give birth and death dates, and can lead you to other family members.
3. Newspaper articles. Some larger libraries have indexed old newspaper articles by surnames.
4. Marriage records.
5. Church records.

MORTUARY

Mrs. Augusta Boos—Mrs. Augusta Boos, wife of Valentine S. Boos, died Saturday morning after an illness of several months. She was born in Neustettin, Germany, in 1852, and came to this country at the age of nine years. She was married in 1883 in Brooklyn, to Mr. Boos and had lived in Saginaw since 1890. She was a member of the Ladies of the East Side Arbeiter society and of St. Johns Evangelical Lutheran church. She leaves her husband, two daughters, Mrs. S. Paquette of Detroit and Mrs. N. A. Gibson of Chicago; one son, Edwin V. Boos of Saginaw; two sisters, Mrs. F. Campbell of Wellfleet, Mass., Mrs. E. Israel, Elizabeth, New Jersey; and two brothers, Emil Roasch, Brooklyn, N. Y. and Fred Roasch, Elizabeth, New Jersey. The funeral will take place from the residence, Monday afternoon at 3:30 oclock. Rev. Frederick Volz will officiate and burial will be in Forest Lawn.

Illustration 4.3

6. Information from published county and city histories.
7. Wills. Some libraries have will abstracts on file.
8. Names of other people researching the same line. Often libraries and societies will keep a surname file with a list of people interested in those surnames.

9. Family histories. In rare and wonderful cases, someone may have written your family up (as I did the Gibson family) and given the history to the library or society.

As you can see, this is an avenue well worth pursuing. In my own research, it is one of the first steps I take whenever I trace an ancestor to a new location. There are a few basics that you need to follow when engaging in this kind of correspondence, however:

1. Be specific. Don't say "Send me all you have on Tom Dixon." Enclose a family group sheet filled out to the best of your knowledge. Tell them that they may keep it for their files. Mark in red the people you are particularly interested in. In your letter, write their names in caps and ask for the details you want—i.e., obituary, cemetery records, newspaper articles, marriage information, county history biography, etc.

2. Offer to pay for copying and reasonable research expenses. I have never yet been charged the latter, but paying for copies is almost always required.

3. Send a self-addressed stamped envelope.

4. Request that if they are not the proper person or institution to address with this matter that they refer you to someone who might be willing to help you.

5. Send a follow-up thank-you letter.

6. Send an updated copy of your pedigree and family history to the library, once the portion of it they would be interested in is complete. This may eventually put you in touch with other relatives, as well as increasing the library or society's resources.

Remember my bio sheet on Adolphus French in Chapter Three? My first action step toward achieving my goal was to "Write Mary Herr at Scott County Library to try to get death record for Adolphus and marriages for Adolphus's other children." Mary Herr is another librarian who has pulled rabbits out of hats for me.

The letter I wrote is shown in Illustration 4.4. In response, she sent me Enos French's marriage record in Scott County, as well as records for four of Adolphus's daughters from across the Mississippi in Rock Island County, Illinois.

Things don't always go so smoothly. When I first began my French research in Kalamazoo, where Adolphus's daughter Vira Ann (my third great-grandmother) was married, I received some cemetery records

```
2 May 1992

Mrs. Mary Herr
Special Collections
Davenport Public Library
321 No. Main St.
Davenport, IA 52803

Dear Mrs. Herr:

Some years ago, you were able to help me with inquiries into my
Jonas Barber family who were early pioneers in Davenport.
Jonas's wife was Vira Ann FRENCH, and when they moved to
Davenport, they apparently brought her unmarried sisters with
them.  Enclosed is a group sheet for Vira Ann's family.  Could
you please check the marriage record index for these people?  I
would also be interested in any cemetery or probate records for
her father, ADOLPHUS FRENCH.

I will be happy to pay any fees for research or copies.  Thank
you so much for your help in this matter.

Sincerely,


G.G. Vandagriff
Address
Telephone Number

Enclosure: SASE
           Family Group Sheet:  Adolphus French
```

Illustration 4.4

from a volunteer in the Kalamazoo Public Library that made a mess of my carefully constructed bio sheet. There appeared to be a serious discrepancy in the information regarding Vira Ann's brother, Ethan French. It seemed there were two people by this name—Vira Ann's brother, born in 1808, and another Ethan I couldn't account for who was buried in Virgo Cemetery. The cemetery record showed that the Ethan French who married Matilda Hounsom on January 1, 1833 (see Adolphus's bio sheet in Chapter Three) was buried with her and their son Clarence French, but the dates on this Ethan French's headstone were 1792–1847!

Had I jumped to conclusions assuming that the Ethan French who married Matilda was Adolphus's son? Perhaps he was a brother? At this Ethan's birth, Adolphus would have been only nine years old, a little young for fatherhood. The fact that both Ethans had died the same year, 1847, further muddied the waters.

I had no alternative but to put a big question mark beside Ethan's name while I looked further into the matter.

So, you say, what does it matter? Ethan isn't on my direct line. The

ADOLPHUS FRENCH

1783: born on 8 Dec in Mass.
1805 (circa): married Annis Grinnell in Mass? Both born Mass.
1810: Living in Tully, Onondaga County, N.Y.
1812-1816: Births of Permelia, Vira Ann, Cordelia, N.Y.
1816: bought lot 21 in Tully from Levi Foster.
1817-1820: Births of Enos, Wealthy, Mary, N.Y.
1818: Sold thirty-nine acres to J.B. Eggleston.
1820: was living in Spafford, Onondaga County, N.Y.
1822-1827: Births of Sophia, Louisa, Lorenzo, Judson, N.Y.
1828: Death of Judson French.
1830: Birth of Amanda French 21 June.
      Six weeks later, Adolphus shown on 1830 Census
      in Orleans County with Enos only. Where was everyone?
1831: Death of Lorenzo French (Feb), death of Laura
      French (Aug), death of wife Annis (Dec).
1833: Marriage of Ethan French Jan 1 in Kalamazoo, Mich.
      Was this Ethan Adolphus's son or brother?
1834: Marriage of daughter Permelia, Kalamazoo, Mich., 2 Oct.
1835: Marriage of daughter Vira Ann, Kalamazoo, Mich., 1 Nov.
      Death of Permelia French Vickery on 18 Nov.
1836: Marriage of daughter Wealthy, Kalamazoo, 14 Oct.
1840: Vira Ann and Jonas Barber living in Princeton, Scott, Iowa.
1843: Marriage of daughter Louisa, in Rock Island, Ill.
1844: Marriage of Sophia in Rock Island, 24 Oct.
      Marriage of Mary in Rock Island, 14 Nov.
1845: Marriage of Enos in Scott, Iowa, 1 Apr.
1847: Death of Ethan French (Jan).
      Both Ethans died this year.
1849: Marriage of Amanda in Rock Island, 1 Mar.
1850: Death of Adolphus on 27 Apr.

QUESTIONS:
1. Where did Adolphus come from in Massachusetts
2. Who were his parents?
3. Did Adolphus accompany Vira Ann, Wealthy, Permelia, and Ethan
   to Kalamazoo after the death of Annis?
4. Who was the Ethan who was1 born in 1792 and married Matilda?
5. Where was Adolphus in 1840?
6. Where did Annis and Adolphus die?

ACTION:

1. Do census search and other investigation on Ethan.
2. Track descendants of Ethan and Matilda French
3. Track descendants of Adolphus.

Illustration 4.5

answer is that we never know what is going to matter in the long run. As it turned out, when I solved the mystery of the two Ethans I was able to solve the mystery of Adolphus French's parentage. More on that later!

Adolphus's new bio sheet (Illustration 4.5) reflects the problem of the two Ethans, as well as the new underlined information I obtained from Mary Herr, the census, and the land records discussed above. I have also made new goals.

FIVE

Using the Census as a Building Tool

And he shall turn the hearts of the fathers to the children, and the hearts of the children to their fathers . . .

—Malachi 4:6

Possibly the single greatest boon to a genealogical researcher in this country is the U.S. census. Because of rapid westward migration, churches found it difficult to keep up with the growing frontier. Marriages were often performed by traveling ministers or justices of the peace. Much of the time, babies went unchristened, and old cemeteries have crumbled, disappeared, been built over, and forgotten. This lack of reliable church records for much of the country during its early years, coupled with sporadic or no state record-keeping, means the census is often the only family record in existence.

Imagine an old white frame farmhouse belonging to one of your ancestors in 1850. It is late spring, and the men are in the fields. Perhaps a spring shower has begun, and your second great-grandmother is scurrying around the house, shutting the large double-hung windows, when she sees a stranger ride up on his horse. From his saddlebag he takes an enormous black book, and with this under his arm, climbs up the steps of the porch. Your ancestor is a friendly body, so she invites him in out of the rain and asks him his business. He is the census-taker. Opening the great book so she can see it, he shows her the entry he has just made for her neighbor over the ridge.

Your second great-grandmother takes the stranger's dripping coat, hangs it in the hall, and invites him into her small parlor with the petit-point chairs. He begins asking her questions, and writes the answers in a large flowing hand upon the pages of his book. "Who is the head of the household? His race? Age? Birthplace? What is the value of your property? Your husband is a farmer?"

She answers the questions about her husband, and then he begins on her. Perhaps she fudges a little about her age, patting the hair in its coil on the back of her head. After they are through with her, he proceeds to her children, and she names each one with pride.

His work complete, the stranger blots the wet ink, then closes his great book, dons his coat, and rides away. Your second great-grandmother goes back to her soap-making and thinks no more about the visit.

The scene changes. Now it is you who are the main character. In quest of this second great-grandmother who is said to have done the petit point on the chairs you inherited, you have come to the National Archives. You have her daughter's (your great-grandmother's) name and her birth date and know the state where she was born, but you do not know her parents' names. In an 1850 index of her birth state, you find several families who have the same last name as your great-grand-mother. Each of them lives in a different county, so you obtain the rolls of microfilm for all of them. Beginning with the first roll, you thread it through the reader and forward the film to the page specified in the index. Nope. No great-grandmother in this family. The names are different, and the ages far too young. You try the second roll, and so on, and then suddenly *there she is.*

On a microfilm copy of the record made by that census-taker over one hundred and forty years ago on a rainy June day, your great-grandmother is listed, as a child of ten, with her seven brothers and sisters and their ages. At the head of the family are your second great-grandparents. Your heart begins to pound. You have just connected yourself to two people you never knew before. This entry on the census is the result of that short interview all those years ago. Could your second great-grand-mother ever have imagined that you, one of her considerable posterity, would see her name in that book? To her it was just a normal day. But because of her actions on that day, you have found a lost part of you, another generation on your pedigree, two more voices in your blood.

Since 1790 when the first census was conducted for the purpose of apportioning the elective seats in the House of Representatives, the census has been taken every ten years. Currently all the censuses from 1790 to 1920 are in the public domain, with the exception of the 1890 census, which was almost totally destroyed by fire.

Where can you go to read a census? First check your public library to see if it has an interlibrary loan arrangement with a facility that

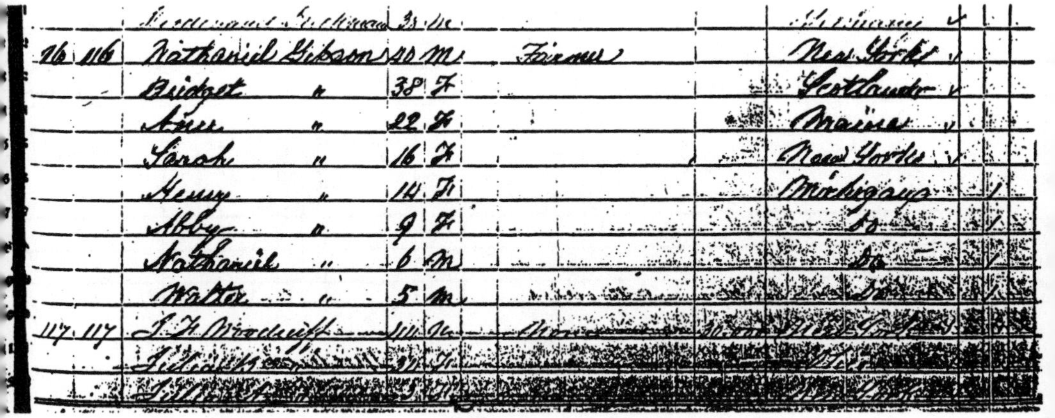

Illustration 5.1

lends the census. My tiny little library does. For $1.34, I can order any reel of census film (reels are designated by county) for a period of one week. If such an arrangement does not exist in your area, search Appendix D at the back of this book for a listing of census repositories.

There are few thrills equal to finding your family names written in the census-taker's bold hand on forms dating back through the last two centuries. Illustration 5.1 shows the first census record I found—that of my second great-grandfather, Nathaniel Gibson, his wife, and family. When I saw it, my heart leapt. If you are sitting in the archives or a library that circulates the census, you will invariably hear muffled (or not so muffled) cries of joy, as someone near you finds his family.

Learning to Use the Census (1850–1870)

The census can be used many different ways in your research. Take a few minutes to study Illustration 5.1. Now! Put on your deerstalker hat, whip out your magnifying glass, and take a closer look. What can you deduce? Illustration 5.2 shows a form used for extracting census data—the form you would use if you were copying information off a microfilm. From it you can see the appropriate column headings for the census record (including columns left blank by the census-taker in Illustration 5.1).

The year of the census is 1850. This is the first year when whole households were listed by name, age, and occupation. This census was

Page No. _____   1850 CENSUS — UNITED STATES   Microfilm
                                                                              Roll No. _____

SCHEDULE 1.   Free Inhabitants in _____ , in the County of _____ , State

of _____ , enumerated by me on the _____ day of _____ , 1850. _____ Ass't Marshal

Line No. on page	Dwelling house No.	Family Number	The name of every person whose usual place of abode on the first day of June, 1850, was in this family.	Age	Sex	Color	Profession, Occupation, or Trade of each male person over 15 years of age.	Value of Real-Estate owned	Place of birth	Married within the year	Attended School within the year	Over 20 who can-not read & write	Whether deaf & dumb, blind, in-sane, idiotic, pauper or con-vict.	(Remarks)

Illustration 5.2

taken on the first day of June, 1850. All dates and information are as of that date. It shows the "free" inhabitants (slaves were not listed) in Saginaw, County of Saginaw, Michigan. The numbers to the left of Nathaniel Gibson's name enumerate dwellings and families. The reason both are given is that sometimes more than one family may have been living together. At the head of the name column, note the description, "every person whose usual place of abode on the first of June, 1850, was with this family." (I had a third great-grandfather in the California gold rush, but he appears on the 1850 census at home in Illinois!) The next columns refer to age, sex, color, and profession of each male over fifteen, value of real estate, place of birth, whether they were married or attended school within the year, and whether they could read and write. The final column asks for designations of special handicaps or conditions: "deaf, dumb, blind, insane, idiotic, pauper, or convict."

Now that you have transferred the data to your extraction sheet, perhaps you have a few ideas about the family. Nathaniel's age looks a little suspicious to start with. If the census is correct, he was eighteen when Ann was born, and Bridget was sixteen. This is possible, of course. I, however, had additional information in the form of the McGill family Bible, which gives Bridget's birth date as January 11, 1809, making her forty-two, not thirty-eight, on the census date. Family Bibles can be wrong, of course, but there is another piece of evidence that makes the census information fishy. Bridget and Nathaniel were married in 1825, which would make Nathaniel sixteen and Bridget thirteen at the time of their marriage! Taken as a whole, the information in the family Bible seems to outweigh the census information, which may have been given by a child.

What else does the census tell us? Consider the birthplaces. New York for Nathaniel, Scotland for Bridget, Maine for Ann, New York for Sarah, and Michigan for the rest. This suggests a rather strange migration pattern—New York to Maine to New York to Michigan. What would have drawn Nathaniel to Maine, surely a rather inhospitable place in 1828? Maine borders on Canada. Was Nathaniel perhaps a soldier? It turns out that he was. By 1850, it would appear that he had retired, however, as his occupation was given as "farmer."

Now let's move on to the 1860 census, where the family was divided onto two pages (Illustrations 5.3 and 5.4). The columns are almost exactly the same, except that the 1860 census added value of personal estate. What do we learn about Nathaniel and his family in 1860? First, that he has become a hardware merchant and that the value of his real estate is $8,000. His personal estate is $5,000. His age seems a little closer to reality, given as fifty-five. Bridget is shown as fifty-one, which is in fact correct according to the family Bible. The children are all shown born in Michigan, which is an error—possibly careless census-taking, as the previous census listed the correct birthplaces. What is most interesting to me, however, are the professions of the children. Sarah (25) is a schoolteacher, Henry (23) is a printer, and young Nathaniel (17) is a clerk, probably in his father's hardware store.

This generates a picture in my mind of a close-knit frontier family, made up of responsible children and hard-working parents. From these two censuses and their brief data we have begun to hear their voices.

Now that you're chomping at the bit to look up your own ancestors, how do you know where to look? The censuses from 1790 to 1850 are indexed on a nationwide basis on microfiche in the Family History Centers of the Church of Jesus Christ of Latter-day Saints. (For information about locating Family History Centers, see Chapter Six.)

I knew Nathaniel was living in Saginaw in 1850, so I looked for him in Search 7a, which indexes all the people living in the United States who were recorded on the 1850 census. Illustration 5.5 shows a photocopy of the fiche where Nathaniel is listed. Even before seeing the census record itself, I was fairly positive he was my Nathaniel, for his residence was Saginaw Township, Saginaw County, Michigan. The number 173 refers to the page number where he is listed on the 1850

23		*Julia W*	"	2	F				"	
24		*Killena S*	"	8m	"				"	
25		*Eliza*	"	44	"		10.000		*N.Y.*	
26		*Joseph Smitty*		17	m	*Gardner*			*Baden*	
27		*Augustus Sibertreib*	23	F	*Servant*					
28	115	685	*Nathaniel Gibson*	55	m	*Hard M Merchant*	50m	500	*N.Y.*	
29		*Bridget*	"	5	F				*Scotland*	
40		*Ann*	"	31	"				*Mich.*	

No. white males, _17_ No. colored males, ____ No. foreign born, ____ No. deaf, ____

No. white females, _21_ No. colored females, ____ No. deaf and dumb, ____

Illustration 5.3

Page No. *93*

SCHEDULE 1.—Free Inhabitants in *Saginaw City* in the County of *Saginaw* of *Michigan* enumerated by me, on the _12th_ day of *June* 1860. *Chas. P. Grant*

Post Office *Saginaw*

| | | DESCRIPTION. | | | VALUE OF ESTATE OWNED. | | | | |
	The name of every person whose usual place of abode on the first day of June, 1860, was in this family.	Age.	Sex.	White, black, or mulatto.	Profession, Occupation, or Trade of each person, male and female, over 15 years of age.	Value of Real Estate.	Value of Personal Estate.	Place of Birth, Naming the State, Territory, or Country.	Married within the year.	Attended School within the year.	Persons over 20 y'rs of age who cannot read and write.
1	2	3	4	5	6	7	8	9.	10	11	12	13
		Sarah Gibson	25	F		*School Teacher*		250	*Mich*			
		Henry	"	23	M	*Printer*			"			
		Oaka	"	19	F				"		/	
		Nathaniel	"	17	M	*Clerk in Store*			"			
		Walter	"	15	"				"		/	

Illustration 5.4

---

census for that county. Knowing that number saves me hours of time that would otherwise be spent reading the census of the entire county, looking for my family.

Archives or libraries that circulate the census may have this index on microfiche, but in the places where I have worked they use the accelerated index system in books designated by state. This means that you cannot make a nationwide search, unless you look up your ancestor in the book for every state. There is one advantage to this state-by-state

```
GIBSON, NATHAN          HAYWOOD CO.           NC 152   NO TWP LISTED          1850
GIBSON, NATHAN <        BLOUNT CO.            TN 095   DISTRICT 11            1860
GIBSON, NATHAN <        DAVIDSON CO.          TN 364   NASHVILLE WARD 3       1860
GIBSON, NATHAN JR.      WARREN CO.            NY 061   QUEENSBURG             1850
GIBSON, NATHAN W.       CHESTERFIELD CO.      SC 146   NO TWP LISTED          1850
GIBSON, NATHANIEL       ADDISON CO.           VT 064   HANCOCK                1850
GIBSON, NATHANIEL       WINDHAM CO.           VT 316   GRAFTON                1850
GIBSON, NATHANIEL       NEW YORK CO.          NY 449   NEW YORK CITY WARD 17  1850
GIBSON, NATHANIEL       BROOME CO.            NY 327   CHENANGO               1850
GIBSON, NATHANIEL       SAGINAW CO.           MI 173   SAGINAW TWP            1850
GIBSON, NATHANIEL       MISSOULA CO.          MT 307   CEDAR CREEK MINES      1870
GIBSON, NATHANIEL       SAGINAW CO.           MI 173   SAGINAW TWP            1850
GIBSON, NATHANIEL       SAGINAW CO.           MI       SAGINAW TWP            1854
```

Illustration 5.5

system, however. The censuses after 1850 have not been indexed on microfiche, but many states have been done separately in book form for 1860 and even 1870. Starting in 1880, a different kind of index called the soundex is used, which will be discussed below.

Uses for the Early Census (1790–1840)

Before 1850, censuses listed only the heads of households and then grouped the rest of the family by age and sex. Though these records are not as informative as the post-1850 documents, they are still useful. It is possible, with a little luck and a lot of perseverance, to find your particular ancestor on a pre-1850 census even when you don't know his father's name. Try using a process of elimination. This worked for me when I was researching my husband David's Vandagriff line.

Family tradition holds that there was a Jacob Vandagriff in the revolutionary war, and that David's second great-grandfather, James, was Jacob's grandson. He was born in Tennessee. You'd think Vandagriff would be a fairly distinctive handle, wouldn't you? Not in Tennessee. There, Vandagriffs grow like weeds. It seems that Jacob Vandagriff migrated to eastern Tennessee after the revolutionary war and brought with him four sons: Leonard, Jacob, Gilbert, and Garrett. Each of these sons had an enormous family of his own, and within twenty years, there were Vandagriffs from one end of the state to the other. Unfortunately, none of them learned to read or write, none of them attended any church that we were ever able to find, and most of them moved on a regular basis as the thin soil of the Tennessee ridges gave out.

A small scrap of paper found with my husband's grandfather's effects told us that James had a brother Jacob. I had been able to locate him on the 1860 census and get his birth year—1827. James was born in 1829. I hadn't a clue as to which Vandagriff family they came from. By 1850, they had apparently left the state, as they were not listed in any of the Tennessee Vandagriff households. No option remained except to try to make some sort of sense out of the earlier censuses.

Conscientiously tracking all the Vandagriffs I could find, I nearly blinded myself copying numbers onto the 1840 census extraction form. At the end of the job, I found that there were three different Vandagriff families who had two boys between ages ten and fifteen in 1840. These were all possibles inasmuch as Jacob would have been thirteen and James eleven in that year. I then went to the 1850 census to try to find these families: G. Vandagriff from Grainger County, John Vandagriff from Anderson, and Leonard Vandagriff from Roane. Both G. and John were successfully accounted for, their families still intact. Leonard, however, appears to have died between 1840 and 1850, which would explain why his sons, now in their early twenties, had dispersed. This makes Leonard the most likely candidate to be my husband's ancestor.

Another use for the early censuses is tracking the movement of ancestors. During those years (1790–1840), few people stayed on the eastern seaboard. For service rendered in the revolutionary war, many received grants from the government to lands that were located in western New York. That area was speedily settled between 1800 and 1830. With the Louisiana Purchase from France in 1803, the new United States of America extended its territory west from the Mississippi to the Rocky Mountains between the Mexican and Canadian borders. Following newly established migration trails, my people moved steadily west during the nineteenth century. Without the census index and a good deal of imagination, I never would have been able to keep up with them.

Migration patterns in the northern area of the United States can be clearly seen using my maternal forebears, the French family, as an example. My fourth great-grandfather, Adolphus, was born in Massachusetts. He appears in his first census as head of household in 1810 in Spafford, Onondaga County, New York. In 1820 he is still there. In 1830, however, he has traveled west by the Great Genesee Road to Orleans County, where he is listed on the census with only one son, Enos. It is probable that he was working as a laborer, endeavoring to support his family.

In 1840, there is no listing for Adolphus at all. However, a taxpayer's list for 1839 shows him living in Kalamazoo County, Michigan, so I know that he migrated across Lake Erie or along the Lake

Shore Path to that state, and then followed the new road that was built through the Kalamazoo Valley in 1829. His son Ethan was the first person to be married in Kalamazoo County on January 1, 1833, so I know that the move was made between 1830 and 1833. I can't yet find any evidence that Adolphus followed his children farther west to the Mississippi.

His children moved steadily westward. By using the census, I was able to track Adolphus's descendants to Iowa, Kansas, Nebraska, and Colorado. The next generation moved farther west, the next farther. My great-grandfather, Adolphus's great-grandson, died in Washington State. There you have the western migration in a nutshell. Today, we take three or four hours to fly across the country. It took my adventurous ancestors four generations of travel through the virgin wilderness to accomplish the same task.

Using the Later Censuses (1880–1920)

Another way to use the census is to travel back in time. Starting with the 1920 census, locate your parents, grandparents, or great-grandparents. To do this you will need to master the soundex code. Illustration 5.6 explains how it works.

When the friend I mentioned in Chapter Two realized she was adopted, we thought we might make a stab at locating the "half" of her that was missing. Jeanne has no frantic desire to meet her biological father, but she realizes that from him she has inherited a genetic legacy that she has passed on to her own children. She had only one small clue as to what that legacy might be. Many years ago, her grandmother had let something slip, saying that she was behaving in a certain unacceptable way because she was Scots-Irish. How could she be Scots-Irish, she wondered? Mom's people were from Croatia and Dad's from Slovenia! Rather a long way from the British Isles. When she discovered the divorce decree and saw that her father's name was Ross, she understood.

We decided to start the search with the 1920 soundex. We didn't know who we were looking for exactly, so we just started with the Colorado soundex for Ross. In order to get his soundex code, we followed the directions in Illustration 5.5, taking the R of the last name, putting a hyphen after it, dropping the vowel o and substituting a 2 for the double s. Because soundex codes must have three numbers, we added two zeroes onto the end. Thus, the soundex code for Ross is

Guide to the Soundex/Miracode System

The Soundex/Miracode filing system, alphabetic for the first letter of surname and numeric thereunder as indicated by divider cards, keeps together names of the same and similar sounds but of variant spellings.

To search for a particular name, you must first work out the code number for the surname of the individual. No number is assigned to the first letter of the surname. If the name is Kuhne, for example, the index card will be in the "K" segment of the index. The code number for Kuhne, worked out according to the system below, is 500.

Soundex Coding Guide

Code	Key Letters and Equivalents
1	b,p,f,v
2	c,s,k,g,j,q,x,z
3	d,t
4	l
5	m,n
6	r

The letters a, e, i, o, u, y, w, and h are *not* coded.

The first letter of a surname is *not* coded.

Every Soundex/Miracode number must be a 3-digit number. A name yielding no code numbers, as Lee, would thus be L000; one yielding only one code number would have two zeros added, as Kuhne, coded as K500; and one yielding two code numbers would have one zero added, as Ebell, coded as E140. Not more than three digits are used, so Ebelson would be coded as E142, *not* E1425.

When two key letters or equivalents appear together, or one key letter immediately follows or precedes an equivalent, the two are coded as one letter, by a single number, as follows: Ke*ll*y, coded as K400; Bue*rck*, coded as B620; L*l*oyd, coded as L300; and S*ch*aefer, coded as S160.

If several surnames have the same code, the cards for them are arranged alphabetically by given name. There are divider cards showing most code numbers, but not all. For instance, one divider may be numbered 350 and the next one 400. Between the two divider cards there may be names coded 353, 350, 360, 365, and 355, but instead of being in numerical order they are interfiled alphabetically by given name.

Such prefixes to surnames as "van," "Von," "Di," "de," "le," "Di," "D'," "dela," or "du" are sometimes disregarded in alphabetizing and in coding.

The following names are examples of Soundex/Miracode coding and are given only as illustrations.

Name	Letters Coded	Code No.
Allricht	l,r,c	A 462
Eberhard	b,r,r	E 166
Engebrethson	n,g,b	E 521
Heimbach	m,b,c	H 512
Hanselmann	n,s,l	H 524
Henzelmann	n,z,l	H 524
Hildebrand	l,d,b	H 431
Kavanagh	v,n,g	K 152
Lind, Van	n,d	L 530
Lukaschowsky	k,s,s	L 222
McDonnell	c,d,n	M 235
McGee	c	M 200
O'Brien	b,r,n	O 165
Opnian	p,n,n	O 155
Oppenheimer	p,n,m	O 155
Riedemanas	d,m,n	R 355
Zita	t	Z 300
Zitzmeinn	t,z,m	Z 325

Native Americans, Orientals, and Religious Nuns

Researchers using the Soundex/Miracode system to locate religious nuns or persons with American Indian or oriental names should be aware of the way such names were coded. Variations in coding differed from the normal coding system.

Phonetically spelled oriental and Indian names were sometimes coded as if one continuous name, or, if a distinguishable surname was given, the names were coded in the normal manner. For example, the American Indian name Shinka-Wa-Sa may have been coded as "Shinka" (S520) or "Sa" (S000). Researchers should investigate the various possibilities of coding such names.

Religious nun names were coded as if "Sister" was their surname, and they appear in each State's Soundex/Miracode under the code "S236." Within the State's Soundex/Miracode code S236, the names are not necessarily in alphabetical order.

Illustration 5.6

R-200. We found the soundex reel that had all the R-200s for Colorado in 1920 and went to work.

We advanced slowly, while Jeanne copied down all the Rosses in Denver that might possibly be her grandparents. Suddenly, she croaked, "Look!" Her eyes round with shock, Jeanne was holding one hand over her heart. I looked at the microfilm and saw a soundex index card for Oscar Ross of Crested Butte, Colorado. "Crested Butte! That's where your mother grew up, isn't it?" I demanded, my own heart pounding.

"Yes." With shaking hands she was already extracting the soundex information onto the extraction form. Critical to our investigation were the enumeration district, sheet number, and line number on the soundex listing, which led us to the precise entry in the census we wanted to find. After obtaining the 1920 film for Gunnison County, Colorado, I forwarded it until I found enumeration district (E.D.) 51.

State:	CO
County:	Gunn.
Township:	Crested Butte
City/Town:	
Ward of City:	

1920 CENSUS
Fourteenth Census of the United States
Enumerated on the _____ day of _____, 1920.
Institution: _____

Date Extracted: _____ FGR No. _____
Depository: Mid-Continent Public Library, North Independence Branch
Microfilm T625 Roll _____ of 2,076 Rolls
Supervisor's District Number _____ Sheet Number _____
Enumeration District Number _____ Page Number _____

Illustration 5.7

Sheet number seven was the one I needed. When I found it, I looked down the page to line eighteen, and there were Oscar, Charolotte, and their family. If this was the right family, my friend's father wasn't born yet, which wasn't surprising. Jeanne's stepfather wasn't born until 1926. Illustration 5.7 shows the complete census extraction form. Notice how much additional information is contained on this census compared to the 1850: relationship to head of household; whether home is rented, owned, mortgaged; marital status; year of immigration; whether person is citizen or alien; year of naturalization; mother tongue; place of birth and mother tongue of parents; whether or not person can speak English; kind of work; and classification of industry.

You can readily see how valuable this information would be, especially items such as year of immigration and birthplace of parents.

Once you have located your ancestors on the 1920 census, look at the year of birth for the head of the household and the state or country where he was born. Oscar was thirty-one, born in Colorado in about 1889, so the next thing we did was start the process over again with the 1900 soundex for Colorado. We knew he would be in a Ross family and that he would show up as a child of eleven or twelve.

Voila! It was easy as pie (Illustration 5.8). Using the soundex information, we found the actual 1900 census entry for Oscar, age twelve, with his parents John and Sadie. There was Jeanne's Scots-Irish blood all right! (See birthplaces of father's mother and mother's parents.)

1900 CENSUS — UNITED STATES

Film Roll No. __124__
State __CO__
County __Gunnison__ }
Township or other division of County __23__
Name of incorporated city, town, or village, within the above named division, __Crested Butte Village__   Ward of City _____
Enumerated by me on the __9__ day of June, 1900, _____ , Enumerator.

Page No. _____
Supervisor's Dist. No. _____ } Sheet No. _____
Enumeration Dist. No. _____ }
, Name of Institution _____

NAME of each person whose place of abode on June 1, 1900, was in this family.	Relation to head of family	Color	Sex	Month of birth	Year of birth	Age at last birthday	Single, married, widowed, divorced	No. of years married	Mother of how many children	No. of these children living	Place of birth	Place of birth of father	Place of birth of mother	Year of immigration to U.S.	No. of years in U.S.	Naturalization	Occupation, Trade or Profession of each person ten years of age and over.	No. of months not employed	Attended school	Can read	Can write	Can speak English	Home owned (free or mortgaged)	Home owned or rented	Farm or house	Number of farm schedule
Ross, John	Head	W	M	May	52	48	M	21			PN	PN	Scotland				Carpenter	6	Ys	Ys	Ys	Y		R		H
Sadie N.	Wife	W		Feb	56	44	M	21	4	4	PN	Ireland	Ireland													
Jessie	Dau			Nov	81	19					PN															
Clarence	Son			Jul	83	16					CO															
Oscar	Son			Aug	87	12					CO															

Illustration 5.8

You can see that the 1900 census is slightly different from the 1920 in ways that are important to the genealogist. It gives number of years married, which can lead you to the marriage certificate and the mother's maiden name. It also lists year of immigration, number of children born to the mother, and number of children living. This last is especially valuable on the 1900 census, due to the loss of the 1890 census. Children could have been born and died in that twenty-year span who would never appear on any census.

Oscar's father, John, was married in Pennsylvania about 1880. This was unfortunate from our point of view, because he might have missed the 1880 census, but we decided to try the Pennsylvania soundex for 1880 anyway. There was a Charles Ross in Crested Butte who might have been Oscar's brother, born in 1879.

With trembling fingers we threaded the 1880 R-200 soundex for Pennsylvania through the machine. We soon had it! There were John and Sadie again with a son Charlie born in 1879 in Armstrong County, Pennsylvania. In the space of a few hours we had gotten Jeanne back to her great-grandfather's home in Pennsylvania.

By ordering church records from Crested Butte, she was able to get Oscar's wife Charolotte's maiden name of Weir, which she needed in order to order her father's birth certificate.

Clues in the census can also help us find our immigrant ancestors' records in the Old Country. Mentioned above is the fact that the 1900 census includes year of immigration. Sometimes more specific information can be found. Remember my Raasch family? My great-grandmother's marriage certificate was illustrated in Chapter Two, giving me the name of her parents—Heinrich Raasch and Florentine (Werth) Raasch. Her obituary (illustrated in Chapter Four) states that she was born in Germany in 1862 and came to this country at the age of nine years, or in 1871. She was married in 1883 in Brooklyn. I therefore deduced that her family would appear on the 1880 census for Kings County, New York.

I chose the 1880 census rather than the 1870 census because there are eighteen rolls of film for Kings County in 1870 and as yet this census is not indexed. Looking the family up in the 1880 soundex, I located them almost immediately.

I don't think I have ever, in all my research, had such a lucky break. Some extremely conscientious census-taker (a German-American, no doubt), *had listed the actual villages in Germany where my ancestors were born.* For census purposes only the country of origin is needed, but for some unknown reason the Raasch's census-taker decided to go the extra mile, at least in their case. No other family on the page has birth villages listed!

When I looked for these villages on a map, they no longer existed, because that part of Prussia is now Poland. My great-grandmother's obituary had stated they were from Neustettin (now Szczecinek, Poland), but the villages on the census—Ratzebuhr, Flatow, and Dummerfitz—actually were not in the city itself, but in the surrounding area. Without the unknown census-taker's zeal, my Raasch line would have been at a dead end.

Of special interest to me were two things: (1) Augusta was not listed with her parents, which meant she was probably working for another family, and (2) Augusta had a little sister named Emily. When I saw the name of this aunt, whom I hadn't even known existed, I sat staring at the screen, blinking back a sudden onrush of tears. There was something very touching about the fact Augusta had named her daughter (my grandmother) "Emily" after this little sister. Shortly after my grandmother's birth, Augusta and Valentine had moved half a continent away from the Raasch family and their shallow American roots to begin a new life in Saginaw, Michigan. I doubt very much whether my great-grandmother ever saw her sister again. Finding Aunt Emily gave me a sense of gathering and reuniting a family that had been separated for many years.

Viewing the page as a slice of Brooklyn in 1880, I was very interested to see that out of fourteen households, twelve husbands and/or wives were from Germany. Their professions were a varied lot: shoemaker, drug warehouse worker (my ancestor), tanner, stonemason, factory engineer, stationer, iron moulder, vest maker, tailoress, press feeder, worker in sugar house, trenchman, clerk in a dry goods store, fur saver, cash boy, house builder, bookkeeper, carpenter.

Can't you just see that crowded Brooklyn street? On June 10, the day the census was taken, I can picture children dodging horse-drawn carts in the dirt street, hailing each other in mixed German and English, while their fathers straggle home from various jobs after a hard day's work. The older generation greet their neighbors politely in German and remonstrate with their offspring using the same sharp commands their parents used on them back in the Old Country. Treasured lace curtains from more-refined European homes blow out the open tenement windows gathering dust from the busy street, while mothers call out urgently that *das Abendessen* is growing cold on the table. These children of the New World leave their play reluctantly, climbing the steps to their cramped rooms and the inevitable sausage and cabbage.

Using the U.S. census is an adventure. You never know what you will find. Some of it might be error with a germ of truth, or vice versa. It is amazing what people don't know about their nearest and dearest. Even their errors can be instructive. Someone in my great-grandfather's family told the 1910 census-taker once that my great-grandfather was born in Colorado. It turned out he had been raised there from the age of three! I hadn't known that Colorado fit anywhere in his past. The mistake was a clue, one that led to the eventual discovery of him on the 1880 census in Colorado, living with his grandparents.

The key to good research is: Find as much as you can about every person you are searching for. Don't be satisfied with one census. Find him on every census you can. Take down the names of the neighbors. They may turn out to be his in-laws. And whatever you do, don't throw anything away!

SIX

Building with Twentieth-Century Technology

As we proceed [with our research] we are joined at the crossroads by those who have been prepared to help us. They come with skills and abilities suited to our needs.

—Boyd K. Packer

In the olden days, genealogy was primarily the hobby of retired professors with perfectly rolled umbrellas and little old ladies in flowered dresses. These estimable individuals pursued their interest with a perfect and finicky patience in dim old libraries, dusty courthouse basements, forgotten, weed-choked cemeteries, and the attics of deceased relatives. If they were very lucky, and saved their pennies very carefully, they might even make a visit to that mecca of meccas—the Family History Library in Salt Lake City. In addition to the largest collection of genealogy-related books and microfilms in the world, that library has an index of over two billion recorded ancestors with birth and marriage dates.

For thirty-five years, my bachelor cousin saved at least a week of his yearly vacation for a trip to Salt Lake City. Lining up outside the library doors before opening time, his day's work planned well in advance, he would be among the first to hit the microfilm machines. With the zeal of Holmes and the method of Poirot, Cousin Bruce would single-mindedly pursue our ancestors, water and candy bars his only sustenance until the library closed. He spent his evenings digesting his finds and plotting the next day's work. When, exhausted and quite a bit thinner, he would return home to Minneapolis at the end of the week, he felt a feeling of deep satisfaction if he had been able to add a couple of generations to the Campbell pedigree.

We don't have to do it that way anymore. For those of us root-diggers who have been led by life to expect prompt gratification of our desires, there is now a better way. Via a CD-ROM data base program called FamilySearch, the Family History Library in Salt Lake has come to us! A computer screen can be our window on the greatest genealogy collection in the world. Using FamilySearch, we can hunt through millions of names in a few seconds to locate our ancestors.

This program is ready for you to use, free of charge, at any of the hundreds of branch Family History Centers of the Church of Jesus Christ of Latter-day Saints where a computer has been installed. In order to find the Family History Center nearest you, look it up in your telephone directory under Church of Jesus Christ of Latter-day Saints— Family History Center. If there is no listing in your town, try the directory for the nearest large city. If you still can't find a listing, call either the number listed for the stake center or one of the local wards or branches of the church near you on Sunday around noon. They will be able to tell you where the closest Family History Center is. If all else fails, you may call the main library in Salt Lake City at (801) 240-2331 and inquire for a list of the Family History Centers. There are over two thousand in existence at the present time, with new ones opening on a regular basis.

Telephone ahead to make certain the center has FamilySearch and also to reserve a time slot for yourself. Some centers are now limiting access to the computer.

When you seat yourself at the computer, you will see the menu shown in Illustration 6.1.

This chapter will show you how to mine the wealth in the Ancestral File, the International Genealogical Index, the Social Security Death Index, and the Military Index. Chapter Seven will be devoted to using the Family History Library Catalog.

Ancestral File

You may, of course, select any of the items on the menu, but my advice would be first to access item B: Ancestral File. Even though it is still in its infancy, this is a miracle of a program. Thousands of people, both members and nonmembers of the Church of Jesus Christ of Latter-day Saints, have submitted their pedigrees to the main branch of the Family History Department in Salt Lake City. As these pedigrees have been received, they have been programmed onto the set of compact disks that are known as the Ancestral File.

```
                              FamilySearch 2.15
   Esc=Exit  F1=Help  F2=Print
                                      ┌──────────────────────────────
                                      │    USING THE COMPUTER
   ┌─────────────────────────────┐
   │     FAMILYSEARCH MAIN MENU   │    "Using the Computer" will teach
   │ Use ↓ ↑ keys to highlight options. │  you the basic computer skills you
   │     Press Enter to select.   │    need to use this system.
   ├─────────────────────────────┤
   │Getting Started               │    You will learn how to:
   │ A. Using the Computer        │     ♦ Move around the system
   │                              │     ♦ Select research options
   │Finding Information           │     ♦ Enter and print information
   │ B. Ancestral File            │     ♦ Respond to computer messages
   │ C. International Genealogical Index │
   │ D. Social Security Death Index │  ├──────────────────────────────
   │ E. Military Index            │
   │ F. Family History Library Catalog │ Help is available throughout
   │                              │    FamilySearch.  When you don't
   │Preparing Information         │    know what to do, press the F1
   │ G. Personal Ancestral File   │    key for help.
   │                              │
   │                              │    ┌─────┐  ┌──┐┌──┐┌──┐┌──┐
   │                              │    │ Esc │  │F1││F2││F3││F4│
   └─────────────────────────────┘    └─────┘  └──┘└──┘└──┘└──┘
```

Illustration 6.1

The chances are good that you will find one of your ancestors already present in this file, complete with pedigree, descendants, and family group sheets. The further back on your pedigree you go, the better the chances are of finding that someone has already uncovered the information you are looking for.

My husband David and I recently had a very rewarding Friday night date with the Ancestral File. When David's grandfather died, his mother forwarded to us a number of items pertaining to the family history. Among them was a copy of an old deed written in copperplate script from the year 1769. Witnessing the deed were John Cooley and Abigail Lippincott. A letter from a distant cousin explained that the deed was that of their ancestor John Cooley. Until our memorable evening at the Family History Center, we had had no luck in our attempts to find John's predecessors. As we seated ourselves at the computer that night, David said, "Okay. Who's being stubborn? Give me a name you can't find anything on." He pulled up the Ancestral File, and I gave him the name and dates on John Cooley. Much to our delight, John showed up in the index with his father, James Cooley. By pressing ENTER, we were able to find more-detailed information. Not only did we see his parents, but there was the mysterious Abigail Lippincott with whom he had witnessed the deed in our possession. She was his wife! After a few high fives, we pressed the F7 key for John's pedigree. Unfortunately, the submitters hadn't been able to go back any further than John's father, but when we looked up the then-newly discovered Lippincott line, we were in clover. Illustration 6.2 shows Abigail's pedigree as it appeared on the screen. The arrows after the end-of-the-line individuals indicate that the pedigree continues further back from those people. By moving the cursor to R. Lippincott, we were able to trace the Lippincott pedigree. In a few brief moments, we had extended David's pedigree from Abigail Lippincott, born 1753, back seven more generations to Edward Lippincott, born about 1541 in Devon, England! Counting all the ancestors branching off from the Lippincotts, David found in one evening five hundred new members of his family.

In addition to pedigrees, the Ancestral File will also show you descendancies up to five generations. We were interested to see the descendancy from Richard Lippincott, so we put the cursor on his name and pushed F8 for descendancy.

What about families? We wanted to see Abigail's family group, so, highlighting her name with the cursor, we pushed F6, and she was shown together with her brothers and sisters as a child in the family of Samuel Lippincott and Mary Preston. The computer also offers us the option of seeing Abigail together with her spouse and children. By moving up and down the pedigree with the cursor, we were able to access family information, individual information, or descendancy information for any of David's new kin.

Now, what about retrieving all this wonderful information? We had two options: (1) printing out the complete pedigree and all the family group sheets, and then going home and entering all the information into our computer by hand, or (2) inserting a diskette in the drive provided, and converting the whole show into a GEDCOM file. GEDCOM is a universal genealogy data base that makes it possible to import or export from compatible software, making it unnecessary to rekey all the information by hand.

Fortunately, we have compatible software in our home computer, so we were able to retrieve the information using GEDCOM. When we took our Lippincott GEDCOM file home on our diskette, we imported those files and linked them onto David's existing pedigree on the hard drive of our computer. This saved us weeks of time. A strike

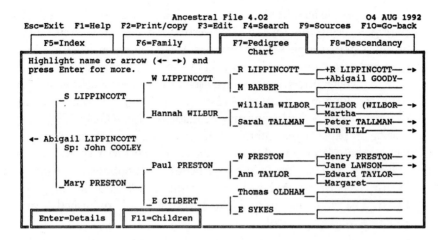

Illustration 6.2

of five hundred names is all very well, until you think of typing in each individual and his vitals by hand!

Another wonderful feature of the Ancestral File is that it can put you in contact with those who are working on the same lines as you are. By pushing the F9 key, David was able to obtain a list of all the submitters who had contributed information to the Lippincott pedigree and its many branches. These were his newfound cousins! People who have submitted to the Ancestral File have done so in hopes that it would connect them with other root-digging relatives. If you find one of your ancestors in the Ancestral File, be certain to take down the submitters' names and addresses and write! They will be delighted to hear from you, and it is even possible that they may have furthered their research since the time they first submitted their data. When corresponding, be certain to send a copy of your descendancy from the common ancestor.

Also, bear in mind that the Ancestral File entries have been submitted by people like yourself. Some of them may contain errors. If your information conflicts, and you have primary sources that indicate that your data is the more correct, you may want to ask the volunteer on duty how to go about submitting a correction to the Ancestral File.

Many people have been unexpectedly delighted as they hit a vein of pure gold using this tool. It is powerful, and will grow even more useful as more people submit their pedigrees. Once you confirm your own pedigree, you should send it in to the Ancestral File. You don't have to go back fifteen generations; even three or four will be valuable to others. By doing this, you can link yourself with relatives from all over the world. Submissions may be made using the GEDCOM format or on paper. Paper submissions can be made on forms that you can purchase at a nominal fee from the Family History Center.

Either way, send your entries to: Ancestral File Submission, Family History Department, 50 East North Temple Street, Salt Lake City, UT 84150. The next time an updated Ancestral File is published, your pedigree will be included!

International Genealogical Index (IGI)

This file, option C on the main menu, contains over two billion names. For years it has been available on microfiche (and still is, in centers with or without computers). The advantage to having it on the CD-ROM is that entire countries can be searched for a name in seconds. Before it was computerized, you could only search the IGI county by county. If you didn't know the county or parish, you were out of luck. Unlike the Ancestral File, the IGI does not link families. You may find all the family members on the IGI, but they will be indexed separately by name and birth date.

The names in this file have been either (1) submitted by members of the Church of Jesus Christ of Latter-day Saints for temple ordinance work, or (2) extracted from church and/or civil records from countries everywhere by a team of specialists.

At this very moment, there are film crews all over the world, sent by the LDS church to microfilm records in churches and state archives of an ever-growing number of countries. I heard the man in charge of this work tell of taking a train to the end of the line in Africa, boarding a canoe, and traveling miles deep into the bush. When he reached his destination, he began interviewing the natives with the aid of an interpreter, taping oral histories of these African tribes who had memorized their genealogies, never having had the benefit of a written language. One day those records will be available in the Family History Library. The people who do this work are truly dedicated and thorough.

Now that the countries in Eastern Europe are opening their doors, many more records are becoming available on microfilm. Copies are stored for posterity in granite vaults in the mountains surrounding Salt Lake City. You may access any of them using the Family History Library Catalog (Chapter Seven).

However, the names on many of these records have already been gleaned and indexed in the IGI by voluntary "name extractors." For instance, almost all available church records in Scotland are now indexed by name on the IGI. The number of names from the British Isles and Germany far exceed those from the United States. So it is certainly worth checking the IGI for an elusive ancestor.

For years I had been trying to find the maiden name of my fourth great-grandmother, who only appeared as Annis on her daughter, Vira Ann French Barber's, death certificate (Chapter Two). There are few things in genealogy as useless as a grandmother's first name. However, one lucky day, I found the maiden name and birth date through the cousin with the Civil War laundry ledger mentioned in Chapter Two.

Climbing into my van, I headed immediately for the Family History Center to hunt for Adolphus French's wife, Annis Grinnell, on the IGI.

The first screen on the IGI lists regions of the world to search. I chose the United States, and then pushing F4, began my search, by typing Annis's name in on the displayed template. I had no idea where Annis was born, so I wanted to search the entire U.S. But if you know that your ancestor lived in a particular state, you may want to zero in on that area by using the filter option (F10), which will show you a list of states (U.S.), counties (England), provinces (Germany, France, Canada), etc. You move the highlight bar using the arrow keys and select your state by pressing ENTER. Whether filtering or not, press F12 when you are ready to search. The screen will prompt you to put a specified CD in the drive. When you have done so, the search for your ancestor will take only seconds. Perhaps you will be as lucky as I was. There on the screen before me appeared Annis Grinnell!

The spelling of her first name was different (Annese), but I had no doubt it was my Annis Grinnell, because the birth date was exactly the same. By pressing ENTER, I received more details. Pressing ENTER again revealed the source. This information had been extracted by a specialist from the Leyden, Massachusetts, town records. The source number shown was the film of the original town records from which this was taken. If I wish to verify it, I may actually order this film and examine a photograph of the page in the Leyden town records that shows this entry. I can even make a paper copy of the microfilm using a reader-printer.

This was a find made possible only by FamilySearch, for I had no idea where to look for Annis. Not even the Grinnell Family Association knew that Patience and Richard Grinnell had a daughter named Annis, or that they ever resided in Leyden, Massachusetts!

Being a greedy genealogist, my next step was to search for Annis's parents' marriage. Pressing F4 to start a new search, I entered the name of Annis's father, Richard.

I found the marriage in Rhode Island. From there it was plain sailing. Our branch library has all the early Rhode Island records on fiche. They also have a set of books giving the ancestry of most early New England families. In the space of one afternoon, I was able to put together a sound pedigree carrying my ancestry back to three *Mayflower* Pilgrims and a French duke! It was an amazing windfall.

Another thing that you can do with the computer that you can't do with the fiche records is to gather families. In order to find Annis's brothers and sisters, I started a new search (F4) and choosing the option that sorts birth information by parents' names, I entered the names of Richard and Patience Grinnell on the template. In a few moments the whole family was gathered before me on the screen.

A friend of mine used this feature another way. She had an ancestor, James McLeish, who was born in Fife County, Scotland. Looking him up, she found that there were many James McLeishes from that county, and she had no idea which one was hers. In her possession she had a letter mentioning two brothers, John and Alexander, who were also born in Scotland. First she printed out all the James McLeishes. Then she took each pair of parents and did a Parent Index search until she found the set of parents who also had an Alexander and a John. In this way, she finally located the right family.

The source shown for your ancestor may have additional information, particularly if the information was submitted by an individual member of the church rather than by extraction.

You can find the individual who submitted this name by ordering the film that is listed as the source document. There will be a batch and a sheet number listed to the left. These refer to submission forms used by the patron who sent in the name. A volunteer will help you order your film ($3.00 rental fee for a three-week period). Make special note of the batch and sheet number. When the film comes, use those numbers to locate the submission form you are looking for. It will have the name and address of the submitter, the source he or she used to find the ancestor, and will often include many other ancestors of yours submitted in the same batch.

If the source is a film of vital records that have been extracted, as was the case when I found Annis Grinnell, you may have located a rich source of information, particularly if it is a foreign source.

In Germany, Britain, and Scandinavia, families tended to stay put for generations. Ordering one film on the parish records of Gau-Bickelheim, Germany, I extracted over two hundred relatives, taking my pedigree back five generations! In this case, only the marriages had been extracted and were in the IGI. Sending for the film gave me access to all the birth and death records.

Other uses for the IGI are limited only by your imagination. How would Holmes use such a wonderful tool?

Social Security Death Index

This program is ideal for detecting the whereabouts of long-lost relatives. Perhaps your family has been rent by divorce and you have lost contact with a grandparent or great-grandparent. You have no idea if he or she is even alive. With this index it is possible to track down deceased relatives who drew Social Security at one time. The index is not complete, so results are not guaranteed, but it is certainly worth a try.

I used the index to find my "Great-aunt" Marie. I last saw her at my wedding in 1972 when she was quite elderly. She wasn't the type of person you forget. In her knee-high black leather boots and floor-length black skirt slit to her thigh, she made a lasting impression on me. It wasn't until I began exploring my family history, however, that I discovered how exactly I was related to her. She is actually a cousin, the daughter of my grandfather's half sister on my elusive Gibson line. I am always anxious to track Gibson descendants, because there are so few. In order to find my Aunt Marie, whom I was fairly certain must be dead, I entered her married name on the Social Security Death Index template, and found a Marie Wouters who had died in Michigan in 1985. Pressing ENTER, I got a more detailed description. Since she had lived all her life in Michigan, I was certain this was my aunt, but I pushed ENTER again to get locality details. The zip code was in Grand Rapids, where she lived, so I was sure I had my lady.

Pushing F5, I brought up the address in Michigan where I could send for her death certificate, using the Social Security death date and place information.

The death certificate, of course, gave me her birth information as well as death information. From this, I could go on to write to a library in Grand Rapids for her obituary, and the cemetery where she was interred for her cemetery records. Thus, I can trace her descendants who might have family Bibles, obituaries, pictures, or other information for me on our common ancestors.

Military Index
This file contains the death records for all servicemen killed in the Korean and Vietnam wars.

As you develop your genealogy skills, you may find other ways of using FamilySearch that no one has dreamed of before. It is extremely flexible and very user-friendly. Don't be afraid to brainstorm, jumping from feature to feature. As time goes on, the files will be updated, and more and more new features will be added to the menu. The Family History Library's aim is to make it possible someday for everyone to have the program in his or her home! FamilySearch is changing the procedure of ancestor detection forever.

SEVEN

Using the Largest Family History Library in the World

I never saw a moor,
I never saw the sea,
Yet I know how the heather looks
And what a wave must be.

—Emily Dickinson

If you had hired Hercule Poirot or Sherlock Holmes to trace your ancestry during the Golden Age of Detection, he would have undoubtedly spent a lot of time traipsing across the world. "These Americans! Don't they ever stay in one place?"

No. That is part of our charm. We take a quarter of this culture, an eighth of that, mix well with Heinz's fifty-seven varieties, and emerge with a unique identity. No two of us are alike. While my brother and sister and I are all half German, an eighth Danish, and three-eighths melting pot, I am the only one who has the imperious Prussian nose and the freckled Danish skin. My sister has a charmingly small nose, fair skin that tans, and long, fine bones. My brother has the Gibson nose, olive skin, and powerful shoulders. We all think and act differently. Our temperaments are as wildly dissimilar as our views of the world. Though born of the same two parents, obviously each of us inherited different genes. We have different voices in our blood.

My voices are not prosaic, prudent, or provident; they are *passionate*. They cry out to me with the deepest emotions in the human spectrum—joy and tragedy. Tchaikovsky, Chopin, Rachmaninoff, Dvořák, Mahler, and Beethoven all speak volumes to the voices in my blood. Central European in temperament, I am not only German, but Slav, a combination that breeds inner turmoil and is responsible for most of the wars on the planet.

When the wall fell in Berlin, I was profoundly moved, as though a barrier were being taken down inside of me. I soared during Bernstein's performance of Beethoven's Ninth Symphony at the Brandenburg gate. *"Freiheit! Freiheit!"* (Freedom! Freedom!), my blood exulted with the chorus.

In Poland, when Lech Walesa finally emerged victorious, and the shackles of fifty years fell from the Polish people, a burden lifted from my own soul. And do I love Mikhail Gorbachev? Passionately.

However, the reality is that I have a husband, three children, and a mortgage. I do not live in Central Europe, but the central United States. Obviously, I can't abandon myself to my passions, dash off to the land of my forebears, and immerse myself in these stirring events. But does that mean I must gag my ancestral voices, eat white bread and baloney? Certainly not.

Because of the efforts of many dedicated people, I can sit in a library not a mile from my brick and shuttered American home and peruse records written on parchment two hundred years ago, rescued on microfilm before Lutheran churches disappeared from post–World War I Poland.

From those microfilmed pages, written in a cramped German hand, I can glean facts that tell of the joys and sorrows of my ancestors. Births, marriages, deaths. As I weave these facts into the fabric of history and human nature, a story grows in my imagination, and I find another part of who I am.

Illustration 7.1 shows a page from the parish records of Ratzebuhr, where the birth of my second great-grandfather, Michael Heinrich Raasch, is recorded at the top of the page. This is my immigrant ancestor, known in the U.S. simply as Heinrich or Henry.

On ensuing pages, the old German script tells me that my fourth great-grandfather was the treasurer of the town of Ratzebuhr, near Neustettin, where he lived in an impressive house with a courtyard, "Polenskahof," married twice, and had twelve children. His daughter, Dorothea Sophia Polenska, married my third great-grandfather, Michael Friedrich Raasch, a burgher and millet-mill owner. She was pregnant with her third child when he died. Within the year, she married her first cousin, by whom she had four more children. Eleven years later

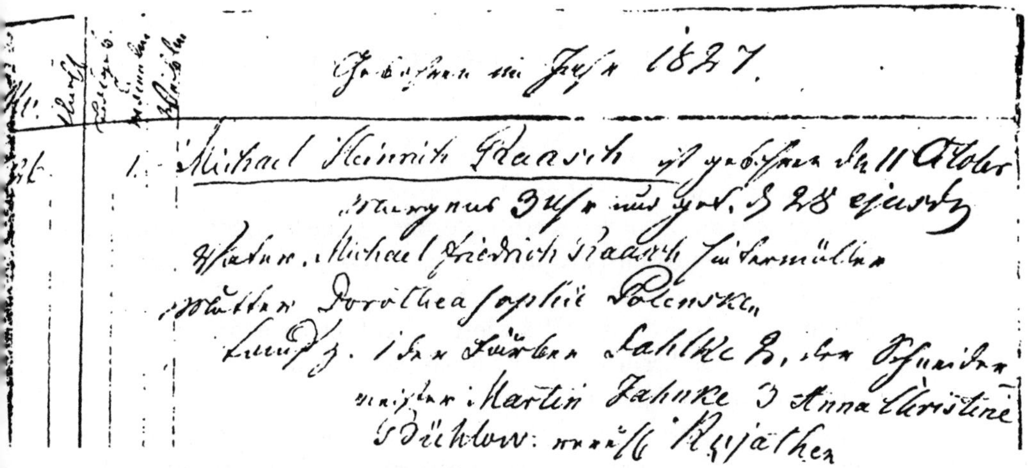

Illustration 7.1

this husband died, and within the year she was married a third time. What a tale can be deduced from those scanty facts!

From these records, I can tell that the Polenska family was a powerful presence in Ratzebuhr, and Dorothea Sophia was related to nearly everyone in town. Her second child, Michael Heinrich Raasch (Illustration 7.1), lost his first wife (a first cousin) and married my second great-grandmother, Florentine Werth, who lived in Polish Wiesneskowa, but attended a Lutheran church in Flatow (now Zlatow).

The couple emigrated to America during Dorothea Sophia's lifetime, taking her grandchildren and leaving the little community where the Polenska roots were spread so broadly and so deeply. What did she think? Did she see her son's leaving as a defection or an adventure? Did he write her from America about his inability to find work befitting his stature in the Old Country? The crowded Brooklyn streets must have seemed a long way from the fertile lowlands of Prussian Pomerania.

It is impossible to describe the exultation I feel when I find my people's names inscribed upon these old records. The closest I can come is to say that it is a reunion of sorts. I am finding someone familiar who was lost to me. I am defining part of myself, solving part of the mystery of who I am. In its own way, it is as stirring as listening to Beethoven's Ninth Symphony.

What makes it possible for me, thousands of miles and two hundred years distant, to hear the voices of these people? The Family History Library Catalog.

Locality Browse

In Chapter Two, I showed you the copy of my great-grandmother, Augusta Raasch's, marriage certificate. She was the daughter of these Pomeranian immigrants, and her marriage record led me to them. In Chapter Five, I showed you how I was then able to find Heinrich and Florentine Raasch on the 1880 census, and how an extraordinarily diligent census-taker had actually listed the town in Germany from which they had emigrated.

My next step was to take the name of this town—written Ratsa-buer—which I was perfectly certain was *not* a German spelling, and try to find it in the Locality Index of the Family History Library Catalog.

To access the catalog, I select option F on the FamilySearch menu. The menu in Illustration 7.2 will appear.

Because I suspected that Ratsabuer was an Americanized spelling, I decided to use Locality Browse. This is a new feature that was not possible when the library catalog was merely on fiche. Like a giant gazetteer, it lists, in alphabetical order, every town or parish in the world for which the library has holdings. Entering that spelling on the template, I scrolled through the resulting names looking for a village in Pomerania that sounded vaguely the same.

I found it! Ratzebuhr! So excited that my hands were shaking, I punched F6 for topics and found that the library in Salt Lake City had a microfilm of Lutheran church records, births, deaths, and marriages, for the years I needed. I filled out my order, paid three dollars, and waited impatiently for the film to be delivered. Without Locality Browse, it would have been extremely difficult to find the right village, for Ratzebuhr is now called Okonck, Kozalin, Poland. The Prussian Luth-eran village of my ancestors has disappeared from the map. All that is left of its congregation are the microfilmed records.

When the film came, it was a mixed blessing. I was prepared for the record to be in German (Lutheran records were kept in the "vulgar" tongue, Catholic records in Latin), but I wasn't prepared for the old German alphabet where *n* looks like *u, c* like *l,* and *s* like nothing on earth. A friend of mine has her doctorate in German language and

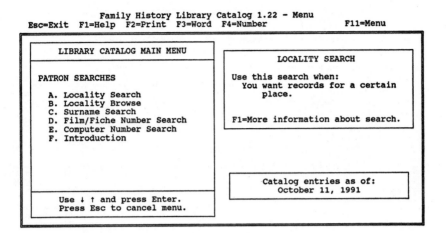

Illustration 7.2

she was extremely helpful, but many times it took both of us to decipher the difficult handwriting. Patience prevailed, however, and after weeks of close study, I was able to take my Raasch/Polenska ancestry with all its intermarriages back another one hundred years. I feel extremely fortunate. Many Prussian Lutheran records have been lost forever.

More records are becoming available all the time, however, and seeming miracles happen on a regular basis. Who would have expected that the records behind the Iron Curtain would become so suddenly accessible? My friend just found that the Family History Center had recently acquired the records from the small town in Croatia where her husband's ancestors came from. She is busy battling Serbo-Croatian and Latin to read the microfilm, and she is winning.

People visiting the Old Country with hopes of gaining access to old church and civil records have been told in many cases, "Go back to your country and go to the Mormon library. The records are all on microfilm. We cannot let the public look at ours anymore, for they are old and falling apart." Before you invest in such a trip, be sure to check the library's holdings!

```
              Family History Library Catalog 1.22 - Locality Search
      Esc=Exit  F1=Help  F2=Print  F3=Word  F4=Number            F11=Menu

       ┌──────────┬─────────────┬──────────────────┬──────────────────┐
       │ F5=Begin │ F6=Topic(s) │  F7=Author/Title │  F8=Full Display │
     ┌─┴──────────┴─────────────┴──────────────────┴──────────────────┴─┐
     │  Topic: All topics                               Page    2 of 3   │
     │  Topic(s) for highlighted area ONLY:        Topic(s) Found: 23    │
     │  Illinois, Rock Island                                            │
     │ ┌────────────────────────────────────────────────Records found─┐ │
     │↑│   12. History                                             6   │ │
     │ │   13. Land and property                                   2   │ │
     │ │   14. Maps                                                2   │ │
     │ │   15. Naturalization and citizenship                      1   │ │
     │ │   16. Newspapers                                          2   │ │
     │ │   17. Obituaries                                          1   │ │
     │ │   18. Periodicals                                         1   │ │
     │ │   19. Probate records                                     5   │ │
     │ │   20. Probate records - Indexes                           1   │ │
     │ │   21. Vital records                                       4   │ │
     │↓│   22. Vital records - Indexes                             1   │ │
     │ └─(More)───────────────────────────────────────────────────────┘ │
     │  Numbers Selected:                                                │
     └───────────────────────────────────────────────────────────────────┘

  ↓ ↑=Move highlight bar    F5=Go back  F6=Change area or topic   F7=Author/Title
  PgUp,PgDn=Change pages    M=Mark/unmark selections               F8=Full Display
```

Illustration 7.3

Locality Search

If the Family History Library has records on the locality you are interested in, you will find the locality listed in the Locality Search or Locality Browse. As mentioned above, Locality Browse acts as a gazetteer. With Locality Search, there is no list provided on the screen. You use this option if you already know the city, county or province, and country you would like to search. Simply fill in the template, and if the locality has been filmed, a list of topics will appear. Illustration 7.3 lists the topics for Rock Island County, Illinois. I am interested in finding a will for Adolphus French, who died in 1850, so I move the cursor to probate records and press F8 for full display. There I see that there is a book of will abstracts for the years 1837–1894 that has been microfilmed. When I order it, it will take between one and two weeks for me to receive it. I will have a period of three weeks to read it before it must be returned. If I wish to extend that time period, I can pay an additional $1.50 and keep it for up to six months.

In addition to vital records, land, and probate records, there are many other wonderful treasures in the catalog—obituaries, county histories, old telephone directories, cemetery indexes, church histories, and military and immigration records. Most books and records have been filmed; some are on microfiche. If the item is only a book, however, you might be out of luck. You can file a request to have the book filmed—but this takes a long time—you can visit Salt Lake yourself, or you can hire a researcher. A word of caution on the last alternative: Rates vary; take a good look through the *Genealogical Helper* (most libraries have a subscription to this periodical) and compare the ads placed there by Family History Library researchers. Some charge an enormous amount.

Surname Search

Besides the locality search, you can also do a surname search. This will list all books or papers in the library that feature a particular surname. When I found Annis Grinnell's pedigree through the Rhode Island Vital Records, I had a whole list of new ancestors. Starting with the name Grinnell, I did a surname search (Illustration 7.4). A book called *Little Compton Families* by Benjamin Franklin Wilbour came up, listing the names of all the people on my new pedigree! It was available on microfilm.

When it came, I found that it gave the genealogies of my people back further than I previously had them. After entering the new names in my computer and printing out my steadily lengthening pedigree, I went back to FamilySearch to check out my end-of-the-line individuals in the Ancestral File. The first one I tried was William Palmer, Annis's mother's great-grandfather.

I had no idea what was in store for me. William's grandfather, Sir Thomas Palmer, had married Catherine Stradling, a woman of "gentle birth." She was descended on her father's line from William the Conqueror, through wicked King John of Magna Carta fame, Edwards I through III, and John "of Gaunt," prince of England and sire of the Tudor line. It seems that John of Gaunt had three illegitimate children by his mistress Katherine De Roet Swynford, whom he later married when the children were in adulthood (see Illustration 7.5). These children, of royal descent, were given the name Beaufort, and it is through them that the House of Tudor descends. My particular ancestor was John's third son, Henry Beaufort, who rose to the height of cardinal in the Catholic church. This did not keep him from reproducing, however. It was his daughter Jane who married into my Stradling line.

All of this was fascinating and exciting to me, as I imagine it would

```
               Family History Library Catalog 1.22 - Surname
   Esc=Exit  F1=Help  F2=Print  F3=Word  F4=Number          F11=Menu
   ┌─────────┐┌──────────────┐┌───────────────┐┌──────────────┐
   │ F5=Begin ││ Add Key Word ││  Title/Notes  ││ Full Display │
   └─────────┘└──────────────┘└───────────────┘└──────────────┘

        ┌─────────────────────────────────────────────────────┐
        │  Type a surname (last name) below. The computer will find the │
        │  number of family histories where that name is prominently │
        │  mentioned in the catalog.                          │
        │                                                     │
        │  Surname: Grinnell_____  │
        │                                                     │
        ├─────────────────────────────────────────────────────┤
        │         Press: key labeled F12 to do the search.    │
        ├─────────────────────────────────────────────────────┤
        │  Press: F1 for help with correcting errors or       │
        │                    truncating when spelling is uncertain. │
        └─────────────────────────────────────────────────────┘
```

Illustration 7.4

be to anyone. My ancestors were part of the history of England, France, Spain—all the way back to Charlemagne. I had heard their names, read about them, even seen their tombs in England. Unable to believe it was really true, I checked the sources, and saw that everything was verified by the Medieval History Unit of the Family History Library in Salt Lake City. I was legitimately an illegitimate descendant of the kings of England.

Still, they didn't feel part of me. I couldn't detect any "royal voices" in my blood. Then I looked closer. Many of the people on this new pedigree were from Wales—Llewellyns, Griffiths, Mathews, Herberts. Then there was King Edward I, who built a string of castles on the Welsh coast to subdue the fiery Welsh, specifically the Llewellyns, the Griffiths, etc. Here was another war inside of me, and another voice given name.

I had just visited Wales the summer before. I knew at the time that there had to be a strain of undiscovered Welsh in me. It was uncanny; I seemed to know what scene was going to appear around each corner, what the vista was going to be from the top of each hill. The whole country haunted me in its familiarity, like a story I had heard long ago in childhood. We visited all of Edward's castles, the most notable being Caernarvon, where Edward II was born. It was rainy and chilly

Ancestral File (TM) - ver 4.02   PEDIGREE CHART   09 SEP 1992   Chart 1

No. 1 on this chart is the same as no. _____ on chart no. _____

```
                                                                              16 Edward II King ENGLAND-
                                                                                 AFN: 8WKN-JD
                                                              8 Edward III King Of ENGLAND-------| BORN: 25 Apr 1284    ___
                                                                AFN: 8XHQ-DT
                                                                BORN: 13 Nov 1312                17 Isabelle P FRANCE------
                                                                Windsor Castle,,, England           AFN: 8XJD-8V
                                                                MAR.: 24 Jan 1327/1328              BORN: 1292           ___
                                              4 John ENGLAND [DUKE OF LANCASTER]- York Minster,Y,, England
                                                AFN: 8XHQ-M2                     DIED: 21 Jun 1377
                                                BORN: Mar 1340                   Shene Palace, ,S, England
                                                A,,, Belgium
AFN=Ancestral File Number                       MAR.: Aft 13 Jan 1396                               18 AVESNES [COUNT OF HAINA
                                                                                                      AFN: 8XQ6-1G
                                                DIED:  3 Feb 1398/1399          9 Philippa Countess Of HAINAULT----| BORN: Abt 1280    ___
                                                L,, England                       AFN: 8XHQ-F1
                                                                                  BORN: Abt 1314                   19 VALOIS [COUNTESS OF HAI
   2 Henry BEAUFORT [CARDINAL]-------                                             Of, Mons,H, Belgium                 AFN: 8XQ6-2M
     AFN: 8XHR-NC                                                                 DIED: 14 Aug 1369                   BORN: Abt 1294/1295
     BORN: Abt 1376                                                               Windsor Castle,,, England
     C,, France                                                                                     20 -----------------------
     MAR.:                                                                                             AFN:
        Not Married                                                            10 Payn De ROET-------------------- BORN:              ___
     DIED: 11 Apr 1447                                                            AFN: 989X-6S
        Winchester,H, England                                                     BORN: Abt 1310                   21 -----------------------
                                                                                  Of, Hainault,H, Belgium            AFN:
                                              5 Katherine De ROET---------------- MAR.:                              BORN:
                                                AFN: 8J5H-L2
                                                BORN: 1350                         DIED:              22 -----------------------
                                                Of, Picardy,S, France                                 AFN:
                                                DIED: 10 May 1403                                      BORN:              ___
                                                Lincoln,L, England            11 Mrs-Payn De ROET----------------
                                                                                AFN: HR9Q-JS                        23 -----------------------
   1 Jane BEAUFORT--------------------                                           BORN: Abt 1315                       AFN:
     AFN: 8XHS-VJ                                                                Of, Picardy,S, France                BORN:
     BORN: Aft 1402                                                             DIED:
        Of, Westminster,, England                                                                  24 FITZALAN [EARL OF ARUND
     MAR.: Abt 1424                                                                                    AFN: 84ZQ-1Q
     Of                                                                                                BORN:  1 May 1273    ___
     DIED:                                                                     12 R FITZALAN [EARL OF ARUNDEL]----- 25 Alice De WARREN--------
                                                                                AFN: 8MLT-WJ                         AFN: 84ZQ-2W
                                                                                BORN: Abt 1303                       BORN: Abt 1277
     SPOUSE                                                                      Of, Arundel,S, England
     Edward STRADLING [Sir]                                                      MAR.:  5 Feb 1344/1345
     AFN: 9F97-PP                                                               , Ditton, , England
     BORN: Abt 1398               6 FITZALAN [EARL OF ARUNDEL,K.G.]--            DIED: 24 Jan 1375                  26 PLANTAGENET [EARL OF LA
        Of St. Donats,H,,, Wales   AFN: 8JDQ-LQ                                                                       AFN: 8TSM-79
     DIED: 1453                    BORN: 1350                                                                         BORN: 1281
        Jerusalem                  Arundel, Sussex, England                    13 PLANTAGENET [COUNTESS OF ARUNDEL- 27 Maud CHAWORTH----------
                                   MAR.: Abt 1365                                 AFN: 8MLT-XP                         AFN: 81Q9-9G
                                   DIED: Jul 1397                                 BORN: Abt 1311/1322                  BORN: Abt 1282    ___
   3 Alice FITZALAN----------------- London,M, England                           G,,, England
     AFN: 8XHS-TC                                                                 DIED: 11 Jan 1372                  28 Humphrey VIII, De BOHUN
     BORN: Abt 1378                                                                                                   AFN: 84ZR-LS
        Of, Arundel,S, England                                                14 William De BOHUN [TWIN]----------   BORN: Abt 1276    ___
     DIED: Bef 1416                                                              AFN: HK72-P9
                                                                                BORN: Abt 1312                     29 Elizabeth, P ENGLAND---
                                                                                Caldecot,N, England                  AFN: 84ZR-MO
                                                                                MAR.: 1335/1338                      BORN:  7 Aug 1282    ___
                                                                                England
                                              7 Elizabeth De BOHUN-------------- DIED: 16 Sep 1360
                                                AFN: 8J5J-L6                                                        30 Bartholomew BADLESMERE-
                                                BORN: Abt 1350                                                        AFN: 8RCP-XP
                                                , Derbyshire, England                                                 BORN: 1275
                                                DIED:  3 Apr 1385             15 Elizabeth BADLESMERE------------- 31 Margaret CLARE--------
                                                                                AFN: 8JDR-CN                         AFN: 8RCQ-01
                                                                                BORN: Abt 1325                       BORN: 1286/1287
                                                                                Derbyshire, Eng.
                                                                                DIED:  9 Jun 1378
```

Illustration 7.5

the day of our visit, but I remember sitting on a stone bench in the middle of the courtyard, feeling peaceful, warm, and lit up inside. I didn't know why then.

I cried when we left Wales. Now, because of the discoveries I made using FamilySearch, I know that I carry a little of it inside of me.

The Family History Library has filmed many old and rare books that are now out of print. Sometimes the item you order will turn out to be a microfilm of loose pages, written in pencil. Sometimes it will be a book of a thousand pages or more taking your family back to the Roman emperors. Either way, surname research can be very rewarding if you observe the caution that what you are reading is a secondary source. Family historians can and do make mistakes, particularly if they are trying to link their family to a prestigious line.

For a short time my husband thought he was descended from Charles Calvert, the third Lord Baltimore who owned vast properties in colonial Maryland. Many books and accounts stated that David's ancestor Mary Calvert, to whom Calvert left "Gunpowder Manor," was his daughter. It seemed obvious, and there appeared, from the evidence, no reason to doubt it.

By this reckoning, David was also the descendant of Anne Arundel, Charles Calvert's mother, which rendered him and all his descendants counts and countesses. For several weeks, David amused all of his relations by calling them up and telling them that by a patent granted to Anne Arundel's ancestor by the Holy Roman Emperor in the 1500s, they were all counts and countesses.

Fortunately, he did not try to borrow money on the strength of this claim, for his life as an aristocrat was short. A very few weeks later we received a letter from a vinegary, but emphatic, genealogist who was researching this line in depth and had proved beyond a doubt that Mary Calvert was Baltimore's stepdaughter only. Dampeningly, she wrote:

> It has been proven that Charles Calvert and Mary Banks Thorpe could not possibly have been the parents of Mary "Calvert" who married your John Chenowith. Charles Calvert had children only by his second wife, and he and the "Widow Thorpe" were not married until 1701, their marriage date being of record in England. Mary was, no doubt, the child of the Widow Thorpe, but NOT Charles Calvert. She was married to John Chenowith in 1704/5 only a few years after her mother married Charles Calvert, and I believe that Charles Calvert treated Mary as if she *were* one of his children! He owned most of Baltimore County, as well as most of Maryland, and deeded grants to his children, including Gunpowder

Manor to Mary and John Chenowith. There are all kinds of things in print about Charles Calvert's land ownership in Maryland and claims of greedy Chenowiths trying to get their hands on some of his estate! The reason they have never been successful was because they had NO LEGITIMATE CLAIM. Some STILL claim to be descendants of the Lords Baltimore, even though it has been PROVEN by records that they are not! People are strange, especially when it comes to relationships to "important people." BIG NAMES. And especially if they think they can get *money* for it!

Despite all this cold water, we paid a wistful visit to Wardour Castle, the Arundel ancestral home in England. David sighed regretfully. The morning was misty and it was such a lovely, spooky old ruin!

However, if you care about having an authentic genealogy, you will always double-check your secondary sources. I have earned the everlasting wrath of a family organization to which I belong, because I proved, at least to my own satisfaction, that their theory about our common ancestor could not possibly be correct. I guess it was my turn to be the vinegary but emphatic genealogist. They did not invite me to the last family reunion.

EIGHT

The Finer Touches

Welcome, O Life! I go to encounter for the millionth time the
reality of experience and to forge in the smithy of my soul the
uncreated conscience of my race.
—James Joyce, *A Portrait of the Artist as a Young Man*

Many genealogists today are satisfied to discover only names, dates,
and places for their ancestors. For a reason that eludes me, their payoff
is in the length of their pedigree. To get back to the earliest records,
those of the Merovingian kings in the fifth and sixth century, is exciting, but what about all the people in between?

A real family historian cares not only for names and dates, but for
personalities. Indeed, it is sometimes impossible to construct a sound
bridge without taking psychology into account. Understanding how
our ancestors think is sometimes imperative in order for us to inter-
pret a bewildering sequence of data.

Reality looks a little different to everyone, our ancestors included.
What is important to Mary may be completely missed by Sam. My
husband refers to the mystery of my Gibson line as "my greatest case."
What makes it most challenging is that every person and every document evince facts that are contrary to one another. The mother's family Bible contradicts the father's, the brother's evidence contradicts the
sister's. Nearly every fact in Nathaniel's obituary conflicts with another source. I have come to the conclusion that in the Gibson family,
facts were communicated mostly by rumor. Exactitude was not perceived as important. It was enough to indicate an idea of the truth.

If we mean to derive full benefit from this study of family history,
we must do more than assemble dates and places. The very lack of
names and places may in itself be a clue to some serious family problem, some need to break with the past. To understand our ancestors
and ourselves, we must somehow arrive at their perception of reality.
This is a tall order.

In order to attempt this feat, we must first see our ancestors as part of the tapestry of history. They did not live in a vacuum. They were part of an age, were players on a landscape we will never see with our own eyes. We must use all the resources available to reconstruct their world view.

Surname Research

One of the most fruitful sources for the kind of personal information we are seeking is other relatives. I'm not talking about the ones we know. I'm talking about the third, fourth, and fifth cousins with whom we share a common ancestor—people we would never find in the normal course of life, people who may possess records and clues that have been passed down to them from our common ancestors. There are several paths we can follow to find these relatives.

I. Ancestral File

Chapter Six detailed use of the Ancestral File. Should you find one of your ancestors in the index, all you need to do is push key F9, and you will find the name and address of the submitter.

My husband had submitted his Swedish ancestors to the Ancestral File some time ago. A distant cousin of his, Albert Lundgren, saw David's name and address, looked up our number, and telephoned. Several days later, we received a beautiful Lundgren family history in the mail. It was lovingly and thoroughly prepared, telling of incidents we had no way of knowing in their common ancestor's life. It had a photograph of her, and by using several historical resources, communicated to us a sense of what her life was like. Anna Lena Peterson's Swedish immigrant voice has become real to us, thanks to Albert Lundgren.

II. International Genealogical Index

Names submitted to the IGI may have been extracted directly from primary-source records or submitted by members of the Church of Jesus Christ of Latter-day Saints. When you find one of your ancestors listed in the IGI, all you have to do is push ENTER twice, and you will find the source of the entry. If it is a member of the church, Chapter Six tells how to order an IGI batch file, which will show the actual photograph of the submitted record, including the submitter's name and address.

III. Family Registry

For several years, anyone using the Family History Library or its branches has been urged to register the names they are researching in the Family Registry. This is a surname file kept in Salt Lake City and distributed on microfiche to all of the branch libraries. If you are able to get to a Family History Center, ask the volunteer to tell you where the Family Registry is kept.

Using a fiche reader, you can examine the registry, which is indexed alphabetically, giving (1) the name of the ancestor; (2) dates and places for birth and death; (3) parents; (4) name and address of the submitter.

IV. Family Organizations

Through the Family Registry, I found the name and address of a person who was interested in starting a Family Organization for the French family. By the time I contacted him, the organization had grown into the thousands. The French Family Association publishes a bound "Yellow Pages" surname exchange once a year, charts of all the known French lines, as well as a newsletter. Every few years there is an enormous French family reunion. Whenever anyone makes a "find," he is encouraged to write in to the FFA and it is put in the computer. It was through this organization that I found my third cousin twice removed who had the famous laundry ledger from the Civil War. There is literally no other way I could have found her or the information she had cherished so carefully.

The Family Registry lists names and addresses for many family organizations. Another way to find one is to ask people that you correspond with. I found the Grinnell family organization by writing to the author of a paper on the Grinnells that I ordered on microfilm from the Family History Library. Also, family organizations are listed in the *Genealogical Helper*.

If there isn't a family organization for your name, start your own! Advertise it in the Family Registry (free) or the *Genealogical Helper* magazine. Use a computer data base to keep track of pedigrees, members, and queries.

V. Roots Cellar

Also available in the Family History Library is a collection of microfiche called the Roots Cellar. This is a listing by surname of all the queries submitted to the *Genealogical Helper* bimonthly magazine.

Very concise, it lists only the name, one event and place, and a number for the submitter. The last fiche is a listing of submitters by number.

I have had excellent luck with the Roots Cellar. Through it I found a cousin still living in Kalamazoo who had been researching my Barber family for years. She was thrilled to find me, as her eyesight was getting poor and no one in her immediate family was interested in carrying on the work she had started. She writes me long letters with all the family news, and has sent me literally reams of material on the Barbers. She is a delight and has become a wonderful new friend.

To Dorothy, our joint ancestors are very real. She still lives a stone's throw from the old Barber homestead. In twenty years of persistent digging, she has found pictures, maps, wills, histories, and descriptions that would never have been available to the casual researcher. Out of this material, she has constructed stories. I feel as though my third great-grandfather Jonas Barber packed me along with him when he trekked west with the forty-niners in pursuit of his fortune. Long letters from his contemporary miners describe conditions in detail, mentioning Jonas and his enterprises. These epistles are a window into the past, chronicling disillusionment and disease, heartbreak and loneliness. From another letter, I learned firsthand, as it were, of the death in the mining camps of Jonas's brother, Parce.

Another rich detail in Dorothy's Barber history was the dying request of Jonas's father, Thomas, who wished to be buried in his apple orchard so that his ghost might frighten away all the delinquent youths who so loved to steal his apples!

My cousin's research has been a delight to me. As a result of it, I can clearly distinguish the Barber in me. I have inherited their salient trait— a love of travel and adventure.

VI. *Genealogical Helper*

This magazine, which I have mentioned several times, primarily exists as an information-exchange resource. People place ads (Illustration 8.1) of all sizes and description, looking for lost ancestors. There is a Roots Cellar index in the back, where you can, for a nominal fee, list the ancestors you are "stuck" on. (This will eventually be filmed onto microfiche and placed in the Family History Centers with the existing Roots Cellar.)

People will write to you from all over the country offering to ex-

July-Aug 1991   THE GENEALOGICAL HELPER. Dedicated to "helping more people find more genealogy"   Page 263

$100.00 Reward To First Person With Documented Proof of Parents of

ELIZABETH ANN MILLS

*   *   *   *   *   *   *   *   *   *   *   *   *   *   *   *   *   *

Mrs. Elizabeth Ann Mills (Mayon) and (Purnell)

Married first probably (?) **Mayon**
Married second Shem **Purnell**
August 1, 1846 in St. Louis, Missouri

Three children born in St. Louis

Emma - died young
Shem Jr. - died young
Elizabeth Ann
and possibly son Brigham / Benjamin

Was in Utah and Idaho in 1855

Divorced Shem **Purnell** about 1858
Joined the Josephite Church
Excommunicated from L.D.S. Church. Church council awarded
custody of daugther, Elizabeth Ann, to father.

Married third Mr. **Williams** (in California?)

They were the parents of three or four children
One son was called Willie

Moved to California

Elizabeth Ann died (murdered) - possibly at age 81 (1909) at
Placerville, El Dorado, California

Contact:

Elva Allen
c / o 825 South 4th East
Providence, Utah 84332

Illustration 8.1

change information with you. You can subscribe to the magazine for $21.00 per year, by writing to the Everton Publishers, Inc., P.O. Box 368, Logan, UT 84321. Family History Centers and Public Libraries will also have copies of the *Helper*.

What makes this publication so helpful is its wide circulation. My own family history has been immeasurably enriched because of an ad placed there by my third cousin, Joyce Lewis. She was looking for descendants of Jonas Barber and Vira Ann French. Through the ad, Joyce and I found one another, to our great delight.

At that time, I was gathering material on Vira Ann for the history in Chapter Eleven. I was particularly wishing I had known my third great-grandmother, for she seemed such an extraordinary woman. I wanted to know what she looked like, what she thought about her life and her remarkable family. I wanted to taste of her experiences and see them through her eyes. At precisely this time, I received a letter from my heretofore-unknown cousin Joyce. She lived only a hundred miles away! We arranged a prompt meeting.

There in a Springfield, Missouri, restaurant I finally saw a picture of my third great-grandmother. The wistful, sad look on her to-me beautiful face tugged at my heart, and tears came to my eyes. Then, while I was looking at the picture, Joyce began to tell stories, and Vira Ann came alive for me in a way she never had before. My cousin's grandmother had been Vira's favorite grandchild, and Vira Ann had wiled away many an hour telling her the adventures she had passed through.

"Did you know when they crossed the Mississippi to go out west, they lashed thirty wagons together on a raft of logs?" Joyce asked me as I stared at the photograph.

"Thirty wagons?"

"That's how many wagons it took to carry all their stuff to Colorado."

"Thirty wagons!"

"My great-grandmother [Vira Ann's daughter-in-law] was there. She used to tell us how amazed she was that no one was hurt and that nothing was lost!"

My great-grandfather had left Colorado and lost touch with this fascinating Barber clan, which has maintained close ties all through the years. The stories about Jonas and Vira Ann French Barber have grown into legend, and it will take some work to separate fact from fancy, but that afternoon I reveled in the love and enthusiasm my cousin felt for these shared forebears of ours and all the outrageous stories she told. Sensing my love and appreciation for our common ancestor, Joyce gave me a quilt block that Vira Ann had quilted by hand, as well as a pair of walnuts from the trees in Colorado that she and Jonas planted.

Finding a cousin who has lovingly collected and preserved memories, stories, pictures, letters—who, in short, shares your fascination in a common ancestor—is nearly equivalent to having the dead speak. They gain in complexity, depth, and personality. When such things happen, a part of the puzzle that is me comes together dramatically. The effect is profound and moving.

VII. *The Telephone Directory*

I have a friend who took a very novel approach to ancestor hunting. Calling Directory Assistance for the area where her second great-grandmother had lived, she got a listing for all the people with the same surname. Dialing each one person-to-person, she asked for her ancestor, who was long dead. At first she had no luck, but finally someone said, "That's the name of my great-grandmother." She called the person back station-to-station and they had a long talk. In this manner, Louise ended up getting her genealogy back several more generations.

I like to use the telephone directory as the final tool in my search for descendants. Anyone who is in the Social Security Death Index (Chapter Six) will most probably have an obituary. By telephoning the library of the town where your ancestor died, you can obtain the obituary, and then use the phone book or directory assistance to find telephone numbers for the survivors mentioned in it. This has yielded me surprisingly fruitful results. These days there is almost always someone in every family who has kept the family history. The person you call might not be the one, but he can usually refer you to someone who is.

By dialing Worldwide Directory Product Sales (1–800–792–2665), you can obtain the directory for any city in the country for a nominal fee. Just calling all of the people in a known area with the same surname you are interested in can oftentimes crack a case.

Be creative! How would Sherlock Holmes have used the telephone directory if such a tool had been available to him?

VIII. *CompuServe*

If you have a personal computer and a modem, you can easily communicate with lots of other ardent family history detectives. A modem is an inexpensive device that acts like a telephone for your computer. With a modem, your computer can call into commercial and noncommercial computer bulletin boards that are devoted to genealogy.

One of the leading commercial genealogy bulletin boards is found on CompuServe. CompuServe contains many different forums, and there is one called Roots that is completely dedicated to family history research.

On Roots, you will see several conversations going on at the same time. Someone will use his computer to post a question—for example, "Does anyone know a source for cemetery records in northern Vermont?" Others who sign onto Roots will see the message and may respond. This is a good place to get quick answers to computer questions. Commsoft, the publishers of Roots III genealogy software, has several employees who monitor the Roots forum and quickly reply to questions about their software.

In addition to the forum messages, there are a large number of files available on Roots for you to download onto your computer. These include such things as a list of organizations that can help with adoption searches, tips on finding missing persons in the United States census, blank genealogy forms, addresses of libraries with records pertaining to the Holocaust, and instructions on how to read abbreviations on faded tombstones. You can start on CompuServe with a CompuServe Starter Kit, available at almost any computer store or by calling 1-800-848-8199.

Military Records

I. *Revolutionary War*

"The next winter . . . I again enlisted for a term of about three months at the court house of Henry County, state of Virginia, about Christmas under Captain Levi Jarvis. We were ordered to guard about five hundred British prisoners which were delivered to us . . . While we had the prisoners we were pursued by the British. We kept along the mountains so as to avoid them and kept our prisoners until we were relieved."

This is the voice of my husband's fourth great-grandfather, Jacob

Vandagriff, describing his service in the revolutionary war. It is taken from the deposition he made in Grainger County, Tennessee, in the year 1833 when he applied for a pension.

When my daughter was studying the revolutionary war in fifth grade, she was able to read this deposition and discover what one of her own kin had to say about the war. For her, the war wasn't just a date in a history book, but part of her own history. Her fifth great-grandfather had guarded five hundred British soldiers, darting in and out of the forests in mountainous western Virginia, avoiding the enemy who wished to free them. Can't you see it? The manacled British prisoners in their soiled red coats, forced to stumble through the rocky American forests in the dead of night, guarded by upstart American volunteers, irregularly clad, but firm in their resolve.

We obtained this record by looking Jacob's name up in the Pension List Index. The Family History Library has it on microfilm, but most libraries with a good genealogy department will have the list in book form. Using the number from the Pension List Index, you can order the pension papers from the National Archives. To do this, you must fill out NATF Form 80. This can be ordered by writing General Reference Branch (NNRG-P), National Archives and Records Service, Eighth Street and Pennsylvania Avenue NW, Washington, DC 20408.

Genealogical information in revolutionary war military records is normally sparse. Age is usually given, but parents and birthplace are usually not. Their primary value lies in the fact that they give us an authentic voice. Reading the testimony of our ancestors, we get a sense of the war as they experienced it.

Whenever a veteran applied for a pension, a file was opened, and into this file were placed all documents concerning that person. Some of the most useful material in the file may be letters written by other people seeking information on that veteran. These letters often lead to other branches of your family who might have a more complete family history.

II. Civil War

Civil War pension records are more helpful genealogically. Illustration 8.2 shows my Uncle Henry Gibson's record, in which he went to great lengths to corroborate his birth date and place. Because of the nature of the deposition, the names of his father, Nathaniel Gibson,

AFFIDAVIT—GENERAL. No. 1153 F. A. Onderdonk, Grand Rapids, Mich.

STATE OF MICHIGAN, }
COUNTY OF Kent } ss.

In matter of Claim of Henry Gibson late of Co I. 2nd Regt Mich Infty Vols who

being duly sworn, depose and say In reply to circular letter under date of Aug 22nd 1907 relative to my Birth.

On the 11th inst I received from Mrs Kate Mc Cullen my neice who resides at No 420 Carlisle St East Saginaw Mich by U S Express the Family Bible published at Battleboro. printed by Fessenden & Co. and Peck and Wood. Boston Mass in year 1834. That under the head or records of births, marriages and deaths. I find that I was born Dec 10th 1836 at Fort Gratiot Mich. That the said record was made at the time of my birth and is the hand writing of my Father Nathaniel Gibson

Henry Gibson.

I, Joseph O. Bellair. a Notary Public. do hereby certify. the above to be a true record from said Bible published in year 1834. in which said record of birth appears. I find no marks of erasure or alteration. To all appearance the record of birth or entry was made at the date given.

PENSION SEP 23 1907 OFFICE

and further th deponent say not.

Affiant

Subscribed and sworn to before me, this 20th day of Sept 1907

Joseph O. Bellair

My commission expires Dec 14, 1910

Notary Public, County of Kent Mich.

Illustration 8.2

and his niece, Kate McCullen, are also given. This document clearly illustrates my point about the Gibsons. The family Bible Henry speaks of was the Gibson family Bible kept by his father. In the McGill family Bible, kept by his mother, it states that Henry was born at Ft. Niagra, New York!

Henry's records tell us that he was enlisted in the Michigan Second Infantry. An account of its service is given in the Saginaw County History:

> The first Michigan regiment to offer its services for three years left Detroit for the field June 5, 1861. Previous to its first service, which was given at Blackburn's Ford, Virginia, July 18, 1861, it mustered 1,115 men. Under General McClellan, it participated in the affairs of Yorktown, April 4; Williamsburg, May 5; Fair Oaks, May 27; Charles City Cross Roads, June 30; Malvern Hill, July 1; and at Chantilly, September 1. In the military report rendered November 1862, it is stated that the strength of the command was reduced to 642 men. At Williamsburg, those placed hors de combat numbered 17 killed, 38 wounded and 4 missing; at Fair Oaks 10 were killed and 47 wounded.

What visions can be conjured from those bald facts! Fifty-six percent of Henry's regiment was killed or severely wounded in the first year. Its opening battles were fought in high summer in the melting Virginia heat. How they must have sweat in their navy blue woolen long-sleeved uniforms! Notice how close together the battles are. The time between would have been spent marching in the heat, treating the wounded and carrying them on stretchers, scavenging for food and good drinking water.

Recently, I discovered that my second great-granduncle, Charles Barber, fought in the Battle of Wilson's Creek, Missouri, a little-known but extremely important battle that saved Missouri for the Union. Wilson's Creek happens to be about thirty-five miles from my home, and I had been there many times before finding out Uncle Charles had fought there.

After receiving Charles's pension papers, I was eager to see the battlefield again. One scorchingly hot day last summer, my family paid another visit to Wilson's Creek, and this time we spoke with the park historian. Because I knew that Charles had served under Colonel Franz Siegel, the historian was able to point out to me the exact ridge where my uncle had stood during the fighting, what he had seen and heard. We were able to visit the Ray House, which had been commandeered by the Union and used as a hospital. Walking the ground that Charles's comrades had soaked with their blood, we came to the hills that had sheltered the Confederate troops. We stood by the innocently babbling creek that, until it was polluted by dead men and horses, had provided their only water on that hot August day in 1861. Knowing my Uncle Charles had fought there, I felt a sense of immediacy about the battle that had been lacking before. I could almost hear the screams of the dying horses, smell the gunpowder, and sense the smoky confusion of war.

The Civil War pension file of a man totally unrelated to me cast some light on a family mystery. One evening a few years ago, I received a call from a stranger who had visited the Davenport Library in order to research his Ganson line. My second great-grandmother, Lucinda Heavlin Barber, had married an Erastus Ganson when her husband, my ancestor Martin Barber, died. The librarian had given the caller my name, and he wanted to discuss what he knew of Lucinda.

"Her son was my great-grandfather," I told him. "When his father [Martin Barber] died, he [my great-grandfather] went to Colorado with his grandmother, Vira Ann Barber. I've always thought it was sad that he lost his father and mother so young. He was only three years old."

"Lucinda's track record was bad," the man said. "The Barbers did the right thing to take your great-grandfather away. She was a real piece of work."

Stunned, and a little affronted, I asked him what he meant. "When Erastus, her second husband, died, she tried to get a widow's pension," he replied. "He was in the Civil War, you know."

I hadn't.

"So was her third husband, Gardner. She tried to get a pension out of him, too."

"What happened?"

"She couldn't prove Martin Barber died! Her second and third husbands' families accused her of bigamy. It's all there in the records.

They must have an eight-inch stack of documents in the archives. Don't send for it all, you could never pay for it."

"But what happened to Martin, my second great-grandfather?" I asked. This was the family mystery. No one seemed to know.

"Her version of it is in the record. I have it somewhere."

He said that he would send me the documents, and with great impatience I awaited the arrival of his letter. Unfortunately, it only contained the first page of her deposition. Just when she was getting to the good part, it ended, and my correspondent didn't know what had happened to the rest of it.

Describing in great detail what I wanted, I filled out a form requesting George Gardner's (Lucinda's third husband's) pension file from the National Archives. Eventually it came, and I had my answer in Lucinda's own words:

After my marriage to Martin J. Barber, we lived on his farm 2 miles east of Hampton . . . for a period of 10 years. Five children were born to us, but only two are living. He died in the year, 1879. He and I were never separated nor divorced before his death. He died in Memphis, Tenn. of Yellow Fever. He had consumption and we went south every winter and would go in a houseboat, drifting down the river. We went to Memphis, Tenn. nearly every winter and would come back in the spring. The last year we stayed there. We went down in the fall, two years before he died, and lived on the houseboat most of the time and stayed in a tent in the edge of the town of Memphis. He had plenty of money and paid 40 dollars a month for a tent to live in. Then in the fall of the year, 1876 I was going to become a mother and he sent me to his mother in Rock Island County, Ill. He sent me and our child—three children had died—back to Rock Island and he was going to dispose of the boat and come back as soon as he could dispose of it. I had not been gone three days when he was quarantined on account of Yellow Fever. His mother got a letter from somebody, I think a minister, but I do not know what it said. I could not read and she got the letter and she felt so badly she never wanted to talk about him. She offered $1000 for his body but they said they would not dare to send it. She got the letter in the spring of 1877.

Q. Why did you or why did she think he was dead?

A. Because he would have come home if he was not dead. He and I never had a cross word and there was no reason why he would not want to live with his family. Then they wrote he was dead.

Q. Who wrote he was dead?

A. I don't know only just what they told me and his mother was just as good and kind as could be and offered to take me with her to Colorado.

Q. But you tell me you do not know what the minister wrote and that his mother, who got the letter, did not tell you what was written?

A. Well, she did tell me, but I cannot remember.

Q. When was the letter written and when was it received?

A. It was in March 1877, I think. My baby was born in November and I know she was quite little. He must have died of consumption if not of fever.

Q. You have previously stated that Barber died in the year 1879?

A. It is a mistake and I should not have said it, if I did. He died in the year 1877 but we left the farm in the year 1879. Now that is wrong and I will get things more confused than they are. I was married the second time in the year 1879 . . ."

Family mystery solved?

III. *Other Records*

The revolutionary war and the Civil War are the best known of the early American wars, but my second great-grandfather, Nathaniel Gibson, was a regular soldier during the years 1821–1837. During those years there was a constant threat from the British along the Canadian border, where he served most of his time. There was also the legendary Black Hawk War where hardly a shot was fired, and the most deadly enemy proved to be not the Indians, but cholera. Inglorious though his service may have been, Nathaniel's records tell me something about him. I know that he was fresh-complected, gray-eyed, stood five feet eight-and-a-half inches, and had brown hair. His enlistment papers (Illustration 8.3) finally provided me with the only reliable clue I have to his birthplace. His obituary claims he was born in Cazenovia, New York, but this has proven to be as unsubstantial as most Gibson "facts." With the military record, at least I have the satisfaction of knowing that it was *Nathaniel* who gave the information. He says he was born in New York City. His discharge papers also give

Illustration 8.3

his age, thirty-three in 1837, proving that in this case at least the obituary was correct. He was born in 1804, not 1801 as his headstone states.
From his bounty-land warrant application, I learn that Nathaniel received 120 acres for his service in the Black Hawk and Florida wars.

Military records may not provide solutions to your most pressing
questions, but they can certainly be used as a supplement that adds

definition to the portrait of your ancestor. Records that can be obtained from the National Archives are:

1. Revolutionary war pension records.
2. Bounty-land warrant applications granted to revolutionary war veterans.
3. Regular army records.
4. "Old wars" (between revolutionary war and Civil War) pension records.
5. War of 1812 pension records.
6. Indian Wars pension records (conflicts between 1817 and 1898).
7. Mexican War pension records.
8. Civil War records—Union forces.

The more completely you fill out the form, the better your chances are of getting the records you desire. I have sent my forms back over and over again, each time adding a new piece of information. In every case, I have finally succeeded in getting what I wanted, so don't be afraid to try more than once.

To request photocopies of records relating to World War I, World War II, or subsequent service, write to: National Personnel Records Center (Military Records), NARA, 9700 Page Boulevard, St. Louis, MO 63132.

Immigration Records

At some point, every American genealogist comes up against the problem of immigrant ancestors. Where was their ancestral home? As a genealogist you must not only find out which countries your ancestors came from, but if possible where within those countries.

I. Family and Home Sources

For immigrants in the nineteenth and twentieth centuries, it is possible to get this information from a variety of sources. Earlier examples have shown how I was able to find birthplaces for my immigrant ancestors using vital records, censuses, and obituaries. Other sources might be old letters or newspaper articles, naturalization papers, and ships' passenger lists. The best source of all, however, is that old standby—the relative.

When my grandfather died, we were fortunate that his stepmother, nearing the age of one hundred, was still alive. You will recall perhaps from Chapter Two that she came forth and told us her stepson had been born in Russia, but his father had never wanted him to know. Fortunately, this step-great-grandmother was also born in Russia in a neighboring village. She was able to tell us the name of my grandfather's birthplace—Doenhof. She also led us to find other living relatives of my grandfather's mother, the Lohrengels. It was through them that I found the American Historical Society of Germans from Russia.

II. *Ethnic Societies*

This society has proved to be a wonderful resource. It is organized by ancestral village, and a village coordinator acts as a clearinghouse for information from members. I was exceptionally lucky, for a very aged man from Doenhof had drawn a map of the village, even down to the detail of who lived in each house! In my packet from the village coordinator, I also received a map showing Doenhof's exact location in Russia and a stack of stories and recorded memories from residents of Doenhof. All of this has given me an excellent picture of that tiny village on the Volga as it existed one hundred years ago, before my great-grandparents left:

> The church and the school were in the center of town and took up the whole block. The bell tower was three stories high and had three bells. There was a space between the church and bell tower for fire protection. The schoolhouse was on the corner. The schoolmaster and family lived behind the school. There was also a shed for horses. There was also a space underneath the cellar for ice, because the whole village depended on ice. In the summer the deceased were kept on ice for three days and then buried. The three days was of religious concept. In winter the bodies were put in cold storage. They made homemade caskets and carried them on their shoulders on a frame to the cemetery. It took six men for an adult and four for a child . . .
>
> On the same block was a big open space for the marketplace. In the winter they had whole carcasses of frozen meat. Hogs weighed up to six hundred pounds. People needed lard for grabble [scrapple] and other baking and cooking. Large families also had better farm cows. The poor people with goats couldn't keep cows because they couldn't afford feed.

The forehouse and the summer kitchen in the house were not heated. To go to the other parts of the house, you went through double doors. The insulation was walls two-and-a-half feet thick. The ceiling was clay five or six inches thick. It would be twenty-five to thirty degrees for months in the winter. They rode sleds from fall to spring.

The beds were built high. This way the lower bed was pushed underneath. This was for children. The bed had heavy quilts from wool. The older folk had feather quilts. There were no mattresses. They used soft straw. It was soft from being thrashed with stones. The people couldn't sleep in because they had to work. In harvest they worked around the clock . . . (From "Doenhoff as Told by Peter Stoll")

What a priceless picture! The American Historical Society of Germans from Russia maintains a library in Lincoln, Nebraska, housing all the records of this people and as many genealogies as they can gather. The have quarterly "work papers" published with stories, recipes, photographs, essays, poetry, and genealogical tidbits. They also publish a surname exchange, fostering an exchange of information among descendants of immigrant families. Unfortunately, the records of the Doenhof Lutheran church remain in Russia, if the church even exists anymore. Those of my relatives who hadn't emigrated were forced to migrate to Siberia during World War II. Few survived.

Many ethnic groups have similar organizations in the United States. To find one, inquire at an ethnic church, genealogy library, or check the *Genealogical Helper*. Even if you can't get pedigree information, you will be able to glean details that will help you to know those people from whom you were made. Their culture is an important part of your heritage.

III. Foreign Sources

Some of my husband's ancestors came from Sweden. In a genealogy class, he was told that Sweden maintains an emigration bureau, called the Emigrantinstitutet at Utvanrarnas Hus, Box 201, S-351 04, Vaxjo, Sweden. He wrote and discovered that they had a record for his ancestors, the Morgans and the Lundgrens. From this source, he learned that the name Morgan was only taken by the generation who left Sweden. Before that time, the family had used patronymics, or names derived from the father's name. David's Morgan ancestor was actually called Sven Peter Sammuelsson, because his father was Samuel. Another important fact he obtained from Utvanrarnas Hus was that his ancestors had come from the district of Kristdala. An American genealogist had even filed with them a genealogy of the Lundgren family. This was a wonderful surprise.

Other countries have similar bureaus. There are many books published and available in libraries about researching in other countries, and I cannot even pretend to cover them here. Also, the Family History Centers have booklets on file for most countries, explaining the best way to carry out research in each country.

IV. *International Genealogical Index*

A resource that is of tremendous help in locating our ancestors within a country is the International Genealogical Index discussed in Chapter Six. My friend Mary knew only that her ancestors came from Germany. She did not know where, and could not find them on any German passenger lists. Before the advent of FamilySearch it was not possible to search all of Germany for an ancestor, for the microfiche records were indexed by province (Bavaria, Hesse, etc.).

Once Mary had access to FamilySearch, the first thing she did was to search for her ancestor Katherina Barbara Binz's marriage in Germany by using the date she had from her family records. She was jubilant when the computer found it in seconds. The records from their village, Rumbach, Pfalz, Bavaria had been extracted by a specialist and indexed in the IGI. Mary ordered the film for the village church and has found hundreds of her kin listed in the parish records. Once the IGI helps you locate where your people are from, it is usually plain sailing, for people didn't move around as much in other countries as they did in America.

Even if you don't have exact dates for events, you can sometimes zero in on an area by finding people of the same surname. In Germany particularly, certain names were endemic to certain parts of the country.

V. *Passenger Lists*

What about passenger lists? For the period from 1600 to 1820, few such lists have survived. A bibliography of sources for colonial American immigration is given in Appendix E. Records after 1820 are more readily available because the passage of the Immigration Act structured the immigration process and mandated a system of record-keeping. The ships' captains were required to report to the government the name, age, sex, occupation, and country of origin of each passenger. These lists sometimes contained other important information about the passengers as well. Records of immigrants arriving at most Atlantic and Gulf Coast ports from 1820 to 1945 are in the National Archives in Washington, D.C., and in its twelve branch offices (see Appendix D). Some branch offices do not have all the records, so before making a long trip, be certain to telephone and ascertain exactly what is available.

If you are not able to make the search yourself, you can request a search by sending in NATF Form 81, which can be requested by writing to the National Archives, General Reference Branch, NNRG, Eighth Street and Pennsylvania Avenue NW, Washington, DC 20408.

Following is a description of exactly what records the archives possess:

The National Archives has inbound Federal ship passenger arrival records dating back to 1820 for most East Coast and Gulf Coast ports and a few lists dating back to 1800 for Philadelphia. Ship passenger lists in our custody are not complete. Fire, dampness, or other causes destroyed many records in the nineteenth century before the creating agencies transferred them to the National Archives. During the nineteenth century, no law required passenger arrival records to be kept for persons entering the United States by land from Canada or Mexico. No law required the keeping of outbound passenger lists.

Limitations of staff time prevent the National Archives from making comprehensive searches of passenger lists or indexes. We can search indexes if you can supply the following information: (1) full name of the passenger, (2) port of entry, and (3) approximate date of arrival. The following major indexes exist: Baltimore 1820–1952, Boston 1848–91 and 1902–20, New Orleans 1853–1952, New York 1820–46 and 1897–1943, Philadelphia 1800–1948, and minor ports 1820–74 and 1890–1924.

NOTE: *There is no index for New York for the Period 1847 through 1896 inclusive.* Therefore, the National Archives cannot search those lists without more specific information. To search un-indexed lists before 1893, you must supply (1) port of entry, (2) name of the vessel, (3) approximate date of arrival, and (4) name of passenger. For those lists, we can also make a search with (1) port of embarkation, (2) exact date of arrival, (3) port of entry, and (4) the name of the passenger. To search un-indexed lists after 1892, we need (1) the port of entry, (2) the name of the vessel, (3) the exact date of arrival, (4) the full name of the passenger, and (5) the names and ages of accompanying passengers, if any.

The more complete the information you include on your form, the better chance you have of obtaining records. Remember that the 1900, 1910, and 1920 censuses include year of immigration to the United States. This can be of immense help. Glean all you can from home sources to indicate what port of entry your ancestor may have arrived at and what port he might have left from in the Old Country.

VI. *Family History Library*

Many immigration records are also available through the Family History Library and can be found in the library catalog for the United States. Germany kept good records of emigrants, and these are also available in the Family History Library. Check the records for the ancestral home of your ancestor by entering the name of the country on the template and then typing in "Emigration Records."

What Do I Do Next?

Once you have inquired of all the sources given so far in this book, you will either have a fairly complete picture of your ancestor, or you will be convinced that you are stuck. If your picture is coming along nicely, you will want to think about writing a biography or history of that particular person. If you are frustrated with your lack of progress, you will need to take strong measures to break through the logjam. Such obstacles appear at some point in most people's research, but genealogy is not for the fainthearted. Proceed to the next chapter!

NINE

Spanning the Final Gap

When you have eliminated the impossible, whatever remains,
however improbable, must be the truth.
—Sir Arthur Conan Doyle, *The Sign of the Four*

Sherlock Holmes was an outstanding detective because, in modern jargon, he never allowed himself to be limited by paradigms—the habitual way of looking at things. Instead of seeing "facts" as givens in a case, he was never afraid to reexamine them, to look at them from an entirely different angle.

It follows, therefore, that when we are stuck on a genealogical "case," whenever our bridge-building stops just shy of the desired shore, we should apply the method of Holmes. No matter how certain we think we are of our facts, we must be willing to inspect each one afresh, from a different angle. In his book *The Structure of Scientific Revolutions*, Thomas Kuhn demonstrated that almost every significant scientific breakthrough smashed an old paradigm. It is the same in family history. We must make what is called a "paradigm shift" before we can see facts in a new light. This new light will often solve an old problem in a surprisingly simple way.

Example: When I received my second great-grandfather Nathaniel Gibson's obituary, I was thrilled. It was very old (1882) and seemed full of wonderful new information.

First, his birth year, 1801, and his birthplace, Cazenovia, New York. He was in the army, as I supposed, mustered out at Fort Gratiot, Michigan. A list of his children was included, followed by this sentence: "A sister of Mrs. Gibson, Mrs. Stoddard of Milford, survives him at the advanced age of eighty."

The previous chapter demonstrated how the military records contradicted the obituary, giving me Nathaniel's version of the correct information: He was born in 1804 in New York, New York. (Cazenovia undoubtedly has some significance, but what? I have not yet solved the mystery of Cazenovia.)

So, we come to the item concerning a Mrs. Stoddard of Milford. One day when we were at the archives, I had my eight-year-old daughter look up the Stoddards on the 1850 census in Milford and copy the information down. I was interested in the fate of Nathaniel's wife's sisters, and there wasn't a Stoddard marriage in the family Bible.

It was a few days before I looked at the census extraction my daughter had made. It showed Orrin Stoddard, age fifty-two, born New York, a wife Sarah, age forty-six, born New York, and children Harriet, Maria, Nathan, Edward, and Edwin.

Puzzled, I got out the McGill family Bible that belonged to Nathaniel's wife's family. It recorded three McGill daughters: Mary Ann, born 1801, Gibralter; Ann, born 1806, Glasgow; Bridget (my ancestor) born 1809, Glasgow. No Sarah. Not even a hint of a Sarah.

Filing the census extract, I thought no more about it until the next time I reviewed my facts. At that time, it struck me as strange. Who was Sarah?

One Sunday morning, I was curling my hair when the truth struck. The obituary was wrong. (How could I be surprised after so many errors already proven?) Sarah was not Nathaniel's wife's sister. She was *his* sister! I got so excited I began to shake. Hair half-curled, I unearthed the obituary and reread it. All one had to do was remove the "s" in Mrs. and it made perfect sense: "A sister of *Mr.* Gibson, Mrs. Stoddard . . ."

There had been no death certificate for Nathaniel. He died a few years too soon. Maybe I would be luckier with Sarah.

Writing to Oakland County, I inquired for a death certificate. As the days went by, I could hardly contain myself. Was I right? Was Sarah Nathaniel's sister? Would they have a death certificate? Most importantly, *would it have their parents on it?*

When the envelope came I tore it open impatiently, and then shouted a triumphant *"Yes!"* Sarah Stoddard had died December 23, 1885. Her father was Nathan Gibson. Her mother was Sena. I was exultant! This is the only record I have ever been able to find of their parents.

What are your stumbling blocks? Try some of the following ideas if you are stuck:

1. Test all the facts by trying to verify them from another source.
2. Look for things that don't make sense, seem uncharacteristic, or even fantastic.
3. Throw out the family legends and have another look at the facts.
4. Look at the family legends from another perspective. Perhaps they contain a grain of truth, if not the absolute truth. Play with possibilities.
5. Use every technique you can think of to trace other descendants.
    A. Surname Organizations
    B. Census
    C. Obituaries
    D. Social Security Death Index
    E. Advertisements in surname publications or *Genealogical Helper*
    F. Roots Cellar
    G. Family Registry
    H. Library in area where they lived
    I. Telephone directory
    J. CompuServe Genealogy Bulletin Board
6. Make certain you have obtained every available document about your end-of-the-line person:
    A. All censuses
    B. Birth, marriage, death records
    C. Church records—confirmation, baptism
    D. Mortuary records
    E. Obituaries and other newspaper accounts
    F. City or town records
    G. Land records
    H. Probate records
    I. City and county histories
    J. Cemetery records
    K. Immigration records
    L. Military records
    M. Naturalization records
    N. Divorce or other court records
    O. Family records: pictures, journals, books
    P. Professional records, e.g., licenses, ledgers, memberships in professional organizations
    Q. Lodge or club membership records

7. Gather as many of these documents as you can for siblings of your ancestor.

8. Look for people of same surname who lived in the same neighborhood as your ancestor on the census. Try to establish relationship.

The most challenging cases will test your ingenuity to the limit, requiring that you use all the tools discussed in this book, and some of your own invention. Rewards in such cases are sweet—the clear light of victory in the battle against the darkness of the unknown. A connection with part of yourself that was hidden.

In the PBS television series "The Creative Spirit," Benny Golson, jazz musician and composer, was quoted as saying: "Creative people are committed to risk. The creative person always walks two steps into the darkness. Everybody can see what's in the light. They can imitate it, they can underscore it, they can modify it, they can reshape it. But the real heroes delve into the darkness of the unknown."

Be a hero. Go where no one has gone before. "Don't refuse to go on an occasional wild-goose chase. That's what wild geese are for," quipped an anonymous genius.

The most dramatic example of a paradigm shift in my own research led to a major breakthrough. Remember the problem of the two Ethan Frenches I hinted at in Chapter Four? The first Ethan was born in 1792 and died in 1847. He married Matilda Hounsom and had a son Clarence. The second Ethan was the son of Adolphus French (my fourth great-grandfather) and the brother of Vira Ann, my third great-grandmother. This Ethan was born in 1808, and also died in 1847. So? Ethan isn't in my direct line. Why the urgency to reconcile this problem?

The urgency was that the mystery of the two Ethans might be harboring a vital clue. I was trying to trace Adolphus's descendants to find someone who might have information that would lead me to his parents. Since the children who lived to maturity were primarily daughters, I was finding the procedure cumbersome. Besides, the most likely descendants to know about the Frenches were those who still bore the name French. Ethan No. 1 had some known descendants. There were Clarence and his children for starters. Were they my relatives or not?

I got one step closer to solving the quandary when I found Ethan on the 1840 census in Scott County, Iowa, just two pages away from Vira Ann French Barber and her husband Jonas.

The first thing that struck me when I looked up Ethan's name in the U.S. census index was that there was no Ethan French in 1840 anywhere in the country except Scott County, Iowa. Also, according to the deed dates, the Kalamazoo Ethan (Matilda's husband) sold his property in Kalamazoo in 1838. I know that it was about this time that Jonas and Vira Ann moved to Iowa, taking Vira Ann's unmarried sisters with them. It made sense to me that Ethan and Matilda might have moved, too.

Examine the extraction sheet for the 1840 census shown in Illustration 9.1. The wife's age falls into the over 30–under 40 category, which is right for Matilda, who, according to her headstone, was born in 1805. She would have been thirty-five years old. But what about Ethan? He is shown in the same age group—over thirty, under forty. If the date on his tombstone (1792) is right, he should be forty-eight! However, if he is Adolphus's son Ethan (b. 1808), he would be thirty-two, which is the age group shown in the census. Because this Ethan is the *only Ethan French in the country in 1840*, the evidence begins to bear out the theory that the Ethan who married Matilda was also Adolphus's son. But what about the date on the cemetery marker?

I didn't have an explanation, but I became virtually certain that two Ethans were one. I couldn't prove it, however, and the vital statistics for both men seemed unshakable. The birth and death dates for Ethan No. 1 were engraved on a modern memorial marker in a cemetery in Kalamazoo. I had both a photograph and a rubbing of it. The birth and death dates for Ethan No. 2 were from Vira Ann's family record. They were less ironclad, certainly, but made more sense. Adolphus himself was only born in 1783. He couldn't have sired Ethan No. 1 at age nine. And if Ethan No. 1 existed, where was he in 1840?

In desperation, I entered everything I knew about these two men in the Research Data Filer, which is a data base included in the PAF program for problems such as these. Entering each piece of information singly, with its source, I was then able to manipulate the data into chronological order and print it out. The result was Illustration 9.2.

Using this list, I could reconcile everything except the birth dates. The marriage fit, the land sale fit with the move to Scott County, Iowa, and the death dates were the same.

Since the problem was driving me crazy, I decided to pursue what might turn out to be a wild-goose chase. I traced the descendants of

STATE Iowa
COUNTY Scott

1840 CENSUS — UNITED STATES

Microfilm Roll No. ____

(No. 4.) SCHEDULE of the whole number of persons within the division allotted to ____

Name of County, City, Ward, Town, Township, Parish, Precinct, Hundred, or District	NAMES OF HEADS OF FAMILIES (Line on page)	FREE WHITE PERSONS, INCLUDING HEADS OF FAMILIES. MALES: Under 5 yrs.	5 & under 10	10 & under 15	15 & under 20	20 & under 30	30 & under 40	40 & under 50	50 & under 60	60 & under 70	70 & under 80	80 & under 90	90 & under 100	100 & upwards
490	French, Ethan	2	0	0	0	0	1							
488	Barber, Jonas	2	0	0	0	1								

Name of County, City, Ward, Town, Township, Parish, Precinct, Hundred, or District	NAMES OF HEADS OF FAMILIES (Line on page)	FREE WHITE PERSONS, INCLUDING HEADS OF FAMILIES. FEMALES: Under 5 yrs.	5 & under 10	10 & under 15	15 & under 20	20 & under 30	30 & under 40	40 & under 50	50 & under 60	60 & under 70	70 & under 80	80 & under 90	90 & under 100	100 & upwards
490	French, Ethan	0	1	0	0	0	1							
488	Barber, Jonas	0	0	0	3	0	1							

Name of County, City, Ward, Town, Township, Parish, Precinct, Hundred, or District	NAMES OF HEADS OF FAMILIES (Line on page)	FREE COLORED PERSONS. MALES: Under 10 yrs.	10 & under 24	24 & under 36	36 & under 55	55 & under 100	100 & upwards	FEMALES: Under 10 yrs.	10 & under 24	24 & under 36	36 & under 55	55 & under 100	100 & upwards
490	French, Ethan												
488	Barber, Jonas												

by the Marshal of the ____ District (or Territory) of ____ (Page No.) ____

SLAVES. MALES: Under 10 yrs.	10 & under 24	24 & under 36	36 & under 55	55 & under 100	100 & upwards	FEMALES: Under 10 yrs.	10 & under 24	24 & under 36	36 & under 55	55 & under 100	100 & upwards	TOTAL.

NUMBER OF PERSONS IN EACH FAMILY EMPLOYED IN: Mining.	Agriculture.	Commerce.	Manufactures and trades.	Navigation of the ocean.	Navigation of canals, lakes, and rivers.	Learned professions & engineers.	PENSIONERS FOR REVOLUTIONARY OR MILITARY SERVICES, NAMES	AGES

WHITE PERSONS INCLUDED IN THE FOREGOING: Deaf & Dumb under 14 yrs.	Deaf & Dumb 14 & under 25	Deaf & Dumb 25 & upwards	Blind	Insane & Idiots: At public charge.	Insane & Idiots: At private charge.	COLORED PERSONS INCLUDED IN THE FOREGOING: Deaf & Dumb	Blind	Insane & Idiots: At private charge.	Insane & Idiots: At public charge.	SCHOOLS, &c.: *	No. of Scholars	No. of white persons over 20 who cannot read and write.

Form 8-0689 * enter whether University, College, Academy, Grammar School or Primary & Common School, as the case may be.

Transcribed by ____ , ____

Illustration 9.1

```
1. French, Ethan
   Born 1792  (Matilda's husband & Clarence's Father).
   (Headstone, Virgo Cemetery)
2. French, Ethan
   Born New York
   (Son Clarence's 1900 Census data)
3. French, Ethan
   Born 1808 (Son of Adolphus)
   (French Family Records)
4. French, Ethan
   Born New York (Son of Adolphus)
   (French Family Records)
5. French, Ethan
   Marriage 1 Jan 1833 to Matilda Hounsom
   (Kalamazoo County records)
6. French, Ethan
   Son of Adolphus probably residing in Kalamazoo
   with rest of family 1834-1836 when his sisters
   were married. (Kalamazoo County records)
7. French, Ethan
   Land purchase 16 Sep 1834
   (Kalamazoo land records)
8. French, Ethan
   Residing Portage St., Kalamazoo, 1835
   (History of Kalamazoo)
9. French, Ethan
   Land Sale 11 Oct 1837
   (Kalamazoo land records)
10. French, Ethan
    Land Sale 9 Apr 1838
    (Kalamazoo land records)
11. French, Ethan
    Residing 1840 Scott County, Iowa, near Barbers;
    Age of Adolphus's son, wife Matilda's age.
    (1840 Census)
12. French, Ethan
    Death 1847 (Husband of Matilda)
    (Headstone in Virgo Cemetery)
13. French, Ethan
    Death 8 Jan 1847 (son of Adolphus)
    (French Family Records)
```

Illustration 9.2

Ethan French, husband of Matilda, father of Clarence. I knew the names of Clarence's sons from the 1900 census. In the 1920 census, I was able to find one of those sons, Earl French, still living in Kalamazoo with his family.

Census extract in hand, I went to the Family History Center and entered the names of Earl's sons in the Social Security Death Index to see if any of them had died. Sure enough, Clyde French had died in August of 1982. With this information, I wrote to my researcher in Kalamazoo and asked if she could find an obituary for me. She wrote me back, saying she was leaving on vacation, but that there was a Clyde French in the telephone book. She gave me his address.

Not certain whether the Clyde in the telephone book was dead (his widow still using his name?) or alive (a son?), I composed a letter, telling the family who I was and what I wanted—information on their ancestor Ethan.

After a week passed, I decided to telephone. A son of Clyde's answered, and told me, "We gave all that stuff to Uncle Earl. He's the family historian."

"Could you give me his address and telephone number?" I asked, heart pounding. A family historian! What could be better?

I lost no time. Phoning Earl French immediately, I introduced myself as the compiler of the genealogy he had received from his nephew.

At first he was inclined to dismiss my information altogether. We weren't related. He knew nothing about Adolphus French or a family of fifteen children. Then he told me what he knew about his Ethan.

Finally, he said something that made my heart quicken. "Permelia?" I repeated. "Did you say Ethan's sister was Permelia?"

"Yes. She married Stephen Vickery, the county clerk, and died in childbirth a year later."

"Then we have to be talking about the same Ethan!" I told him. "That same Permelia was Vira Ann's older sister! It's in the family records!"

He repeated the information to make certain he had heard it right. Paradigms are not easy to shift. He had someone entirely different in mind for Ethan's father and had never heard of Adolphus. Finally, by reviewing fact after fact, we came to the conclusion that his Ethan was indeed Vira Ann's brother and Adolphus's son. He had moved to Scott County, Iowa, but after losing a child, it appears that the family moved back to Michigan where Ethan died.

There remained one problem, however. I told him. "Wait a minute. There's the headstone."

"The headstone?"

"The one in the Virgo Cemetery. It says Ethan was born in 1792."

"Oh." Silence. Finally, "I put that up. It's not a headstone. It's a memorial. Ethan isn't even buried there. He's buried at Indian Fields Cemetery."

"But the date!"

"Well, I didn't know his birth date. I guessed."

Let that be a lesson to you. I keep a rubbing of Ethan's headstone framed in my office as a reminder that paradigms can be written in stone, and still be wrong!

But after all this fancy footwork, was Cousin Earl able to help me find Adolphus's parents? That's an even better story. Earl maintained that his ancestor, Ethan, was buried with another French—*Enoch*—in Indian Fields Cemetery. They were related, but he was a bit hazy on the details.

Checking out Enoch, I found that he was born in Massachusetts in 1775, married, and migrated west to a town a few miles away from Adolphus's New York residence. He also moved to Michigan at the same time my Frenches did. It was certainly a possibility that Enoch and Adolphus were brothers.

The only "hard evidence" that Earl had about Enoch was that his father was named Jacob French and that he came from the vicinity of Taunton, Massachusetts. Jacob Frenches are very thick on the ground in Massachusetts. Which was the right Jacob? And was he Adolphus's father, too? Enoch's father had been a cobbler. A copy of his cobbler's ledger was included in the papers my cousin Earl sent me. A cobbler's ledger? Hardly the thing to trigger a breakthrough.

But I had an idea. Taking the ledger to the Family History Center, I began entering the names on it in the IGI. Some were common names (e.g., Samuel French); others one of a kind (e.g., Nehemiah Newhall). I printed out all the people with those names born or married between 1720 and 1770 in Massachusetts. The result was very gratifying (Illustration 9.3). *There was one person by each of those names born or married in Berkeley, Bristol County, Massachusetts.* Therefore, the Jacob French I wanted had been a cobbler in Berkeley, once called South Taunton.

I ordered the town records and found him. He had married Wealthy Richmond in 1760. More confirmation! *Enoch French had a son named Richmond. Adolphus French had a daughter named Wealthy.*

Then, from records in possession of the French Family Association, I found that this Jacob French had moved to the area of Orange, Hampshire County, Massachusetts, after the revolutionary war. I was getting warmer. This was a town within a few miles of the town where Annis, Adolphus's wife, was born. The town records in that part of Massachusetts were sketchy and uninformative. (It later came out that the town records I needed were lost in a fire.)

But then I had another piece of luck. A probate index on microfilm for Hampshire County listed estates for Jacob and Wealthy. Writing to the probate court, I got the disappointing answer that the records

International Genealogical Index (TM) - 1988 Edition - Version 2.16

09 SEP 1992   SELECTED ENTRIES   Page 1

Names (Sex)	Event Date/Place	LDS Ordinances	Batch & Sheet	Library Call Number For Source Document
RICHMOND, Perez (M)..................... B: 15 Jan 1744		B: 11 Sep 1928	8306202	1395553
Father: Joseph RICHMOND	Berkeley, Bristol, Massachusetts	E: 10 Apr 1929 SL	15	
Mother: Hannah DEANE		SP: 27 Oct 1983 OK		
WINSLOW, Avery (M)..................... B: 21 Mar 1735		B: Cleared	J584281	903401,903402
Father: Ebenezer WINSLOW	Berkeley, Bristol, Massachusetts	E: Cleared		
Mother: Esther		SP: Cleared		
PHILLIPS, Nathaniel (M)................ B: 20 Jul 1751		B: Cleared	J584281	903401,903402
Father: Nathaniel PHILLIPS	Berkeley, Bristol, Massachusetts	E: Cleared		
Mother: Mary		SP: Cleared		
MACOMBER, James (M)..................... M: 4 Feb 1747		SS: 23 Feb 1949 SL	A456499	456499
Spouse: Rachel DRAKE	Berkeley, Bristol, Massachusetts			
MACOMBER, James (M)..................... B: 18 Aug 1753		B: Cleared	J584281	903401,903402
Father: James MACOMBER	Berkeley, Bristol, Massachusetts	E: Cleared		
Mother: Rachel		SP: Cleared		
NEWHALL, Nehemiah (M)................... M: 6 Apr 1749		SS: Cleared	M584281	903401,903402
Spouse: Hannah BABBIT	Berkeley, Bristol, Massachusetts			
FRENCH, Joseph (M)..................... B: 3 Jun 1766		B: Cleared	J584281	903401,903402
Father: Jacob FRENCH	Berkeley, Bristol, Massachusetts	E: Cleared		
Mother: Welthey RICHMOND		SP: Cleared		
FRENCH, Ephraim (M)................... B: 17 Sep 1744		B: Cleared	J584281	903401,903402
Father: Israel FRENCH	Berkeley, Bristol, Massachusetts	E: Cleared		
Mother: Mary		SP: Cleared		
FRENCH, Nathan (M)..................... B: 23 May 1748		B: Cleared	J584281	903401,903402
Father: Seth FRENCH	Berkeley, Bristol, Massachusetts	E: Cleared		
Mother: Phebe		SP: Cleared		
FRENCH, Ebenezer (M)................... M: 9 Feb 1735		SS: Cleared	M584281	903401,903402
Spouse: Reziah PHILLIPS	Berkeley, Bristol, Massachusetts			
FRENCH, Ebenezer (M)................... B: 27 May 1737		B: Cleared	J584281	903401,903402
Father: Ebenezer FRENCH	Berkeley, Bristol, Massachusetts	E: Cleared		
Mother: Keziah		SP: Cleared		
FRENCH, Samuel (M)..................... B: 4 Sep 1751		B: Cleared	J584281	903401,903402
Father: Samuel FRENCH	Berkeley, Bristol, Massachusetts	E: Cleared		
Mother: Freelove		SP: Cleared		
GOODING, Matthew (M)................... M: 21 Aug 1760		SS: 15 May 1975 WA	7427001	935199
Spouse: Marcy CRANE	Berkeley, Bristol, Massachusetts		52	

Events: B=Birth C=Christening M=Marriage N=Census W=Will A=Adult Chr. D=Death F=Birth of 1st Child S=Miscellaneous
LDS Ordinances: B=Baptized E=Endowed SP=Sealed to Parents SS=Sealed to Spouse

(continued)

Illustration 9.3

were too old to copy. Frustrated, I telephoned the library in Northampton, the county seat. They gave me the address of a librarian, Brian Tabor, who undertook research projects at the courthouse. I wrote to him immediately.

After a few weeks, my answer arrived at last. To my disappointment, Jacob died intestate six months before Adolphus was born, and his estate papers crumbled in my researcher's hands. They were impossible to read. My researcher felt terrible, and as a coda to his letter added, "Also included was the following:"

> Will . . . Wealthy French of Orange, widow, being weak of body but of sound mind and memory . . . this 20th day of May 1797 . . . to my three daughters all my wearing aparel [*sic*] and household furniture to be equally divided . . . and whereas my son Sabinus is not capable to provide for or support himself, I give and devise to my oldest son Jacob French the little farm on which I now live . . . and comfortably to support my said son Sabinus . . . and pay to my son *Adolphus* [!] when he shall arrive to 21 years of age . . . and ordain my said son Jacob French sole Executor.

I couldn't believe my luck. Adolphus's father died before he was born. He was only fourteen when his mother died. Therefore, Adolphus and the incompetent Sabinus needed provision for guardianship, so they of all her children (I eventually found ten), were mentioned in the only legible part of a will that was turning day by day into dust. My long, difficult search was finally at an end!

The next step was easy, because the French Family Association had records on Adolphus's father that took him back to his immigrant ancestor, John French.

This search for Adolphus's forebears was the most difficult I have undertaken to this day. The sense of relief and exultation I felt when I finally connected him with his family was incomparable (Illustration 9.4).

What new things did I learn about my heritage with this breakthrough? I learned that I am descended from the original settlers of Taunton, Massachusetts—the Frenches and the Richmonds. Both are old English surnames dating back to the days of the Norman Conquest. This is my only "real" American line, in fact. Adolphus's father and grandfather were officers in the revolutionary war. On his mother's line, he was descended from the *Mayflower* Pilgrim Thomas Rogers.

ADOLPHUS FRENCH

1783: born 8 Dec near Warwick, Franklin, Mass.
Parents: Jacob French, Jr. (died July before
was born) and Wealthy (Richmond) French.
1797: Mother Wealthy dies in May. Brother Jacob
becomes Adolphus's guardian.
1804: Adolphus turns 21 and comes into his inheritance: his mother's farm.
1805: (circa) Married Annis Grinnell of Leyden, Mass.
1806-1810: Births of 2 sons, 2 daus. Where?
1810: Living in Tully, Onondaga, New York, near brother
Enoch (living Eaton, Madison, New York.)   .
1812-1816 Births of Permelia, Vira Ann, Cordelia, N.Y.
1816: Bought Lot 21, Spafford from Levi Foster
1817-20: Births of Enos, Wealthy, Mary, N.Y.
1818: Sold thirty-nine acres to J.B. Eggleston.
1820: Living in Spafford, Onondaga, N.Y. (census)
1822-27: Births of Sofia, Louisa, Lorenzo, Judson, N.Y.
1828: Death of Judson French
1830: Birth of Amanda French 21 Jun.
1 Aug Adolphus shown on 1830 Census in Orleans Co.,
N.Y. with Enos only.
1831: Death of Lorenzo (Feb). Death of Laura (Aug). Death of
wife Annis (Dec) on way to Michigan. She is buried
in Lake Erie.
1832: Family arrives in Kalamazoo County. Settles in
Arcadia Township near brother Enoch.
1833: Marriage of Ethan French 1 Jan, in Kalamazoo, Mi.
(First marriage in Kalamazoo)
1834: Marriage of Permelia French 2 Oct, in Kalamazoo.
1835: Marriage of Vira Ann French 1 Nov, in Kalamazoo.
Death of Permelia French Vickery 18 Nov, in K-zoo.
1836: Marriage of Wealthy French 14 Oct, in Kalamazoo.
Departure of Vira Ann and Jonas Barber for Scott, Ia.
(Vira Ann takes younger sisters with her)
1839: Adolphus is taxpayer in Oshtemo Twp., Kalamazoo, Mi.
1840: Vira an and Jonas Barber living in Princeton Twp, Ia.
1843: Marriage of Louvisa French in Rock Island, Illinois
1844: Jonas and Vira Ann move to Rock Island
Marriage of Sophia French in Rock Island, Illinois
Marriage of Mary French in Rock Island, Illinois
1845: Marriage of Enos in Scott Co., Ia., 1 Apr.
1847: Death of Ethan French (Jan)
1849: Marriage of Amanda French in Rock Island, 1 Mar.
1850: Death of Adolphus on 27 Apr.

Questions:
1. Where was Adolphus in 1840?
2. Where did he die?
3. Where were Adolphus and Annis married in Massachusetts?

Action:
1. Search for Almira and Cordelia French in Oshtemo, 1850.

Illustration 9.4

From this French line I inherited a colonial ancestry to mingle with
the loyalist ancestry on my father's side of the family. These two sets of
ancestors were real people with passions and beliefs strong enough to
move them to bloodshed. On the battlegrounds of Massachusetts and
New York, these forebears of mine fought one another in the revolutionary war. By studying about them and their traditions, I have

gained a fresh perspective of history, realizing that "patriotism" was not nearly so cut-and-dried as I had believed.

More importantly, however, I have gained self-knowledge. These people are part of the pattern that is me. When I stand back and look at the larger picture, as I will in Chapter Eleven, I can see how the values of these ancestors are built into my own belief structure. As in the case of my Polish ancestors, long before I knew these people existed, they were voices in my blood.

What will you find when you finally complete your bridge? Press on! Remember, there is always more than one way to skin a cat.

TEN

Putting Your Work in Perspective

Praise the bridge that carries you over.
—Traditional African-American saying

Truth takes away fear and fosters understanding. We are links in a chain, rungs on a ladder, planks of a bridge. We are neither the end nor the beginning. We have our own unique place in history. In a sense, we are history—our children's history. When they view our lives and what we have done with them, they will need to understand our times—Vietnam, Watergate, environmental issues, the atom bomb—in order to understand our preoccupations and decisions. And in order to see out of our eyes, they will have to understand our perception of our family and our place in it.

Similarly, in our attempts to put all the planks of our bridge together and assemble a family history, we must view our ancestors in an accurate framework. We cannot endow them with our own historical perspective, our own sense of political correctness, or our religious beliefs. Dr. Laurel Thatcher Ulrich, author of the Pulitzer Prize-winning *A Midwife's Tale*, prefaces her work with the warning: "To understand Martha's world we must approach it on its own terms, neither as a golden age of household productivity, nor as a political void from which a later feminist consciousness emerged. Martha's diary reaches to the marrow of eighteenth century life. The trivia that so annoyed earlier readers provides a consistent, daily record of the operation of a female-managed economy. The scandals excised by local historians provide insight into sexual behavior, marital and extra-marital, in a time of tumult and change . . . The somber record of her last years provides rare evidence on the nature of aging in the preindustrial world . . ."

Our ancestors responded to the age in which they lived in real, human ways. In order to garner their reality and derive a sense of personal meaning from it, we must make an effort to do as Dr. Ulrich says and approach that world on its own terms.

How do we achieve this sympathy? How can we possibly learn what our forebears dared and thought and felt?

First of all, we must rid our minds of stereotypes or personal prejudices. Much as we may desire to meet our own needs for "worthy" ancestors, psychological and historical truth are vital if we are to arrive at an account that is meaningful in the deepest sense. Life is not and never has been simple for anyone. Far more insight is to be gained from an accurate account of real people dealing with real problems than from an idealized portrait of a person with unassailable courage, undaunted faith, or unrelenting optimism.

In his excellent book, *Writing the Family Narrative*, Dr. Lawrence P. Gouldrup, says, "The beginning writer, particularly when he is dealing with members of his own family, often cannot resist the temptation to present family members in stereotypical strokes. Typically he might draw his mother as an angel of mercy and his stepfather as a villain of repression, although in reality both parents fed into and maintained one another's personalities. Moreover, while real individuals alternate between admirable and socially unacceptable qualities (complexity), they are normally a fairly predictable blend of those qualities (consistency)."

Our ancestors were neither all good nor all evil. They were complex creatures, just as we are. Understanding their characters depends on how much of this complexity we are able to uncover.

So how do we do this? How do we historically and psychologically submerge ourselves in the world of our ancestors?

We must move beyond the sources we have used for genealogical identification purposes, take our ancestor off the pedigree chart, and place him in history.

Choose an ancestor whose voice particularly intrigues you. You may not be able to explain your preoccupation with this person, but trust your instincts. As he becomes more real to you, the reason for your feelings will clarify and your eyes will become his eyes.

An excellent place to begin is with a chronology, such as *Time Lines: World History Year by Year Since 1492*, published in 1988 by Crescent

Books. Read about the events that formed the world in the years surrounding your ancestor's birth.

In 1813, the year my third great-grandmother, Vira Ann French, was born, the Napoleonic Wars were at their height. The previous year, Napolean had entered Moscow. In 1813, he defeated the Russians and Prussians and took Dresden, but then was defeated in the "Battle of the Nations" by a coalition of European powers. Wellington initiated a formidable string of victories that were to culminate the following year in Napoleon's exile to Elba.

On the cultural front, Percy Bysshe Shelley completed a controversial poem *Queen Mab*, which expressed his philosophical ideas. The waltz became the most popular dance in Europe, Beethoven was on the ascendant, and the Royal Philharmonic Society was founded in London.

The technology of war was advanced by a Frenchman who devised the first practical cartridge for the .59 breech-loading rifle, while the War of 1812 heated up in the United States. Many American ports were blockaded by the British, who also burned Buffalo, New York. The Americans burned York, Ontario.

What impact would this variety of information have had on the tiny frontier village in western New York where Vira Ann was born?

More than you might think. Because the French family lived in upstate New York where most of the fighting in the War of 1812 occurred, there was a very real concern for their safety. Tremendous uncertainty prevailed as to whether hostile Indians (who had been forcibly removed from their county of Onondaga by the post–revolutionary war army) might side with the British. The Frenches lived in a state of vigilance and fear for their homes and safety.

European cultural events still determined American tastes, even on the frontier. The newspapers, delivered by slow post, contained accounts from London, Paris, New York, Boston, and other cosmopolitan centers. It was the great Romantic Age, and the fact that it penetrated to New York was clearly evident in the names Annis French chose for her children. Three were taken from Shakespeare, one from Lord Byron, and most all the others were fanciful and not in keeping with her Puritan ancestry.

Since both France and the United States were at war with Great Britain, French taste was fashionable, and Napoleon was idealized.

Perhaps because of this, Vira Ann's mother told her children stories about their own noble ancestor who had fled France when he embraced the Protestant faith. This was something Vira Ann was proud of all her life, and the knowledge seems to have had an important impact on how she chose to view herself.

How can we get a sense of our ancestors' immediate surroundings as they viewed them in their day? An indispensable tool for this kind of research is the county history. During the 1800s many eastern publishing companies made a good business out of sending itinerate journalists to frontier counties to create a "county history." The advantage that these works have over modern histories is that the research done for them was conducted among original residents of the counties who were still alive. There are firsthand accounts of such things as wolf hunts, the frontier fever, and wedding customs.

You may have run into these volumes in your searches for genealogical tidbits. Return to them now, and glean what facts you can from the general discussions of life during the time your ancestor lived. These books are a treasure trove for the family chronologist. They add zest to our work, deepening our perspective by placing our family in a definite landscape with a sharply defined foreground and background.

I had always considered that, compared to her Puritan forebears, Vira Ann must have had a culturally deprived upbringing, growing up as one of the first white settlers in western New York. It was extraordinary to me that she was able to read and write. When I began researching the county and town histories, however, I discovered that Spafford, New York, was an extension of the New England village. It was nothing like the rough pioneer settlements that later developed in the West and Midwest. This difference helped me to discern the important distinctions Vira Ann later felt between herself and the denizens of other frontier towns.

In *Writing the Family Narrative*, Dr. Gouldrup recommends asking and answering the following questions about your ancestors:

1. "Where did the family come from and where and *why* did it settle?"

Answering the "why" part of the question is often the most instructive. People tended to migrate in groups. There was usually a common denominator in their reasons for migration. Croatians, accustomed to the rough terrain of the Austrian Alps, chose to farm in the mountains of Colorado, because that is where they felt at home. The open prairie, though more fruitful, was frightening to them in its unrelieved vastness. Scandinavians chose to migrate to the severe climes of the northern Midwest, where the forests and wildlife most closely approximated their homeland. Russian and Eastern European Jews immigrated to ethnic urban neighborhoods, not because of any similarity to their homeland, but because of an intense desire to obtain an American education for their children, while maintaining a religion and society as traditional as the one they had left.

Migrations within the country happened for definite reasons, as well. A study of conditions in the place the family left will often provide a reason. The French family of Onondaga found its economic survival unexpectedly threatened by the opening of the Erie Canal, which brought cheaper wheat and other grains from the west where they were grown in vast quantities. I surmise that the family's migration was dictated by economic urgency rather than a desire for change.

2. "How did the family earn its money and how did it *spend* it?"

Determining occupation is a fairly obvious idea, but it had never occurred to me to wonder how the family chose to spend its money. Inventory lists that accompany wills are probably the best indication of this. Dr. Gouldrup compares the estate inventories of two of his ancestors and draws from them very illuminating conclusions about their differing characters, homes, and values. Until I thought about inventories in this way, I had never bothered to look at one!

3. "What did the family consider important or valuable?"

Certainly part of the answer lies in what society in general valued at the time. Did your family pull with or against the tide? One of the things that makes Vira Ann such a fascinating creature to me is that not only was she raised differently from other girls of her age and class, but she chose to uphold these values against all the assaults frontier life could make upon her. Not only does this conflict deepen her character for me, it actually provides the energy behind my narrative and the point at which her life touches mine.

What religion did your ancestor profess? What were its central values? What were the burning issues of the day in his part of the world and what were his opinions upon them?

4. "What kind of social standing and personality patterns did the family exhibit?"

My Raasch great-grandmother, Augusta, always took tremendous pride in her social standing and status. She was "Prussian." Migrating to the United States in the days of Bismarck at the height of the Prussian empire, she felt indisputably superior to other immigrants, even non-Prussian Germans. In the old country, her family had been of the upper middle class—her father the son of a mill owner, her grandmother the daughter of the town treasurer. When she married in the Brooklyn German community, it was to another immigrant, a literate typesetter who was the son of a German newspaper editor. Her husband eventually went on to edit his own German-language newspaper in the German community of Saginaw, Michigan. These parents brought my grandmother up to believe she was a privileged young woman of impeccable heritage who must maintain an elevated standard of behavior.

What is very interesting, however, is that Augusta's sisters married quite differently. One married a machinist from Elizabeth, New Jersey, the other a poultry farmer from Massachusetts. Augusta's perception of herself and her status was obviously enhanced by the choices she made. What about her sisters? How did they feel about their Prussian heritage? They married middle-class Americans. My guess is that they did not pass the same cultural/familial pride on to their children. They handled life in the new world differently, by absorbing themselves into the new culture and taking on its values. The sisters appear to have lost touch with one another almost entirely.

Good sources for social information are the census, land and court records, old directories, and county histories. What were the occupations of other people in the community? How much land did your ancestors own and what was the value of that land? What size farm was considered average and what size above average? If they were not farmers, what social standing did they occupy in their day by virtue of their trade or profession? What were their politics? Were they often in court? What about their children? What trades did they follow? Who did they marry and what did that signify about their parents' social position?

Local histories explode the myth that early American society was classless. For many years, until frontier life reduced men and women to their basic essence, the English class system prevailed in the colonies. The Industrial Revolution in the nineteenth century brought about a new class system. Not until after the Civil War did the idea of "landed gentry" finally disappear.

Answering the question of your ancestors' social status is vital for an understanding of his or her self-consequence. A knowledge of one's place in the overall scheme of things was much more important in the past than it is in today's more mobile society. It is impossible really to hear the voice of an ancestor, if we don't understand where that voice is coming from.

For extensive bibliographies and sources that might help you in your quest to answer these questions, I refer you to Gouldrup's book, *Writing the Family Narrative*. Another, more personal source is available to you in family memorabilia, particularly photographs.

Try doing a detection exercise based on a photograph of an ancestor. You will be amazed at how much you can deduce. A tintype of my husband's great-grandfather, Joseph Callaway Vandagriff, shows him standing behind his two brothers, Jake and John. Their jocular, informal poses, unbuttoned vests, loosened ties, carelessly tilted hats, and worn boots suggest a trio of "good ol' boys" from Tennessee, aggressively masculine, fond of a good time, and free of the need to make a genteel impression. It is a very telling photograph, and from what I have been able to gather, accurately reflects the personalities of the subjects.

Now consider this: a photograph taken twenty to thirty years later. The subject is obviously a young man of sober habits and careful attention to his personal appearance—starched white collar, meticulously barbered hair, conservative, formal attire. He is, in fact, a clergyman in the making. What is harder to fathom, and what makes these two pictures so fascinating, is that the Joseph Callaway Vandagriff of the first picture is the father of Joseph Earl Vandagriff, the subject of the second. What is the story behind the transformation that occurred from one generation to the next?

When you finally get to the point of bringing all your newfound wisdom and the facts you have gathered into some type of form or story, it may appear to be an overwhelming task. How can I organize all this mass of detail, all these unrelated facts? How can I fill the gaps? What can I do to make this person live?

The first thing to do is to reconstruct your ancestor's life, seeing things in terms of cause and effect. Remember that whenever some action took place—for example, selling the family farm—it was done for a reason. Search for the reasons behind the actions. What was going on in the county, the country, the world? How did your ancestor deal with events? And most of all, how did his response to the conflicts in his life determine the legacy, for good or ill, that he left for you and the rest of his posterity?

Once you have answered these questions, the work will begin to structure itself. The next step is to search for a theme, a thesis that will shape your biography for maximum impact. Ask yourself the question: *Why do I feel so passionate about this person?* Because he or she is like me? Because he or she has qualities I wish I had? What are they?

Once you have zeroed in on these feelings, determine the stories you have gathered that most closely define your ancestor in terms of your passion. At this point, a theme should begin to emerge.

Conflict is the engine that will drive your theme through your writing. Look for those events that provided the opposition in his or her life. How did he or she handle them? Remember, no one wins all the time, so don't intentionally overlook your ancestor's defeats or setbacks. We learn much about a person from his reaction to opposition.

Keep in mind the three basic conflicts that provide thematic material in all good writing: man versus man, man versus environment, and man versus himself. In reality, our life includes all of these struggles. Looking at your ancestor's life, can you distinguish which conflict appears to you to be the overriding one? Did that predominate conflict change over time? Is there any recurring fear or drive that seems to dictate his or her decision-making? Are these same fears or drives present in your own life?

This last question brings us to the crux of the matter. What does it mean to you to be descended from this person? Have you learned anything about yourself from deciphering the details of your forebear's life? Have you determined what part of your identity you owe behaviorally, materially, or genetically to this person?

To review—in organizing your material thematically, you will consider the following questions:

1. What is the cause-and-effect relationship behind the events in your ancestor's life?
2. Why do you feel so passionate about him (or her)?
3. What traits and/or events in your ancestor's life define him in terms of your passion?
4. What events provided opposition in his life?

5. What was the central conflict that seemed to rule him?
6. What does all this mean to you?
7. What legacy has this ancestor left you?
8. What have you learned about yourself from your understanding of your forebear's life?

Attempting to answer these questions honestly, while viewing your ancestor in his unique historical framework, crowns your research, lending a particular vision that cannot be achieved in any other way. As you draw parallels between your forebear's life and your own, surprising truths will emerge. You will feel a healing oneness between yourself and this person as you relate to his hopes and dreams, challenges and disappointments.

Then, like Llewellyn's character quoted in Chapter One, you can stand in a line that stretches from Time That Was, to Time That Is, and Is Not Yet, raise your hands to show the link, and find that you are one.

ELEVEN

Hearing the Voice

The following is the beginning of a biography of my third great-grand-mother. Illustrating how all of the techniques in this book can culminate in the creation of a detailed, three-dimensional portrait, it also draws important parallels between her life and mine, identifying our common voice.

When I first encountered Vira Ann, she was only a name on a census—V. A. Barber. Now she is a defining presence in my life.

Frontier Ballad

Born on the edge of the frontier in 1813, Vira Ann was raised by parents of staid Puritan stock. Their roots went deep in colonial America. Her father Adolphus French's forefathers crafted a "New England" out of the hostile wilderness of the New World. Conservative by nature, but also independent and opinionated, the Frenches had slowly evolved into revolutionaries, breaking with Mother England and casting their lot with those visionaries who would begin a neophyte nation of their own.

Annis Grinnell French, Vira Ann's mother, was of a mixed heritage. The Grinnells descended from an idealistic young Huguenot who had renounced the comforts of noble birth for his faith, fleeing to England and then to America. Sympathetic to the Pilgrim cause, Matthew Grinnell emigrated to New England, where his children intermarried with disaffected *Mayflower* descendants who had left the rigid life of Plymouth to found a gentler colony in Rhode Island. In their little colony by the sea, Annis Grinnell's people prospered, intermarrying with the same old families for one hundred and sixty years, never forgetting their past.

Annis and Adolphus's parents were the first to break with tradition, leaving their ancestral homes for new settlements in northwestern Massachusetts after the revolutionary war. After marrying, Annis and Adolphus decided to leave New England altogether, migrating to the new county of Onondaga in central New York. They proved to be the transitional generation, providing their children with the benefits of the Puritan ethic, at the same time freeing them from the rigidity of the Puritan environment.

Of course, Annis and Adolphus didn't realize the role they were playing. For them it was enough that there was a wilderness to tame, a new settlement to carve out. They saw themselves doing what their forefathers had done, creating a "new" New England. In the year preceding Vira Ann's birth, her father Adolphus had attended Spafford's first town meeting, where he was made commissioner of highways. This new settlement was no rough encampment, but a town laid out according to the New England model, with religion and education given first priority. Churches built in the New England style crowned the picturesque ridges that rose above the two defining lakes—Skaneateles and Otisco. A town government was established according to the two-hundred-year tradition that had steered colonial America.

America was again in the midst of war with England, a war fought this time principally along the New York–Canadian border, and settlers in Onondaga were uneasy. Buffalo was burned by the British, and ports along Lake Ontario were in constant danger of British bombardment. What mainly concerned the Onondagans, however, were the Indians. Would they join forces with the British, as they once had with the French, and raid the new, defenseless settlements?

At the time of Vira Ann's birth, her parents were understandably uneasy. Would this war force them to abandon their new home and move again? Adolphus decided to wait the situation out before investing his savings in land.

Despite such ever-present anxiety, life went on. Vira Ann came into a busy world where the steady hack of settler's ax was felling an ancient forest of hemlock, beech, maple, and pine. The air was redolent with tree sap and wood chips. These sights, sounds, and smells of civilization being wrought out of wilderness were to be ever present in her life, the strong warp threads through which all her other experiences were woven.

In the nine years since her marriage, Annis French had already borne five children. Vira Ann was the sixth, coming just eighteen months after her sister Permelia. In naming her fifteen children, Annis departed from the solid Puritan appellations meant to remind their bearers of duty. The names of her girls were gentle and delicate, suggesting flowers— Almira, Permelia, Vira Ann, Cordelia, Sophia, Louvisa, Amanda—a strange contrast to the rugged wilderness that surrounded them. Only Wealthy bore a name out of the past, in honor of Adolphus's mother. Another daughter, Laura, bore the newly popular name of the heroine in Lord Byron's poem *Don Juan*. The boys' names were more traditional to begin with—Adolphus, Jr.; Ethan (after the revolutionary war hero Ethan Allen); and Enos. Eventually, however, Annis bestowed fanciful names on her male children as well. The last two were called Lorenzo and Judson.

Annis's fancies reflect the Romantic spirit of her times, which penetrated even to western New York. It was the age of Wellington and Napoleon, Shelley and Byron, Beethoven and Rossini, the waltz and the quadrille.

Imbued with a special sense of her name, Vira Ann seemed to gather from it all that her mother intended. She was definitely not out of the Puritan mold. In fact, she had a concept of her own importance unusual for a middle child in such a large family. In later years, manifestly proud of what she considered her superior heritage, education, and cultural attainment, Vira Ann always declared with great dignity that she was born in "York State." Though her adult life was rugged in the extreme, she managed to preserve a distinct vanity and decorum. How did she develop such an exalted view of herself growing up in what can only be described as humble circumstances? This strong sense of self-worth must have been nurtured by Annis.

In 1816, after the Indian threat had subsided, Adolphus finally purchased a forty-five-acre lot in Spafford for five hundred and seventy dollars. He was a farmer by profession, and that first summer on his own farm would prove a very disappointing one, for it was the infamous "cold season," with snow in May and a heavy frost on the ninth of June. Food commanded enormous prices. For example, at one period in midsummer flour reached the price of $16.00 per barrel. Throughout the entire region many families suffered for lack of food, the Frenches surely among them. The family pot was filled with fruit of the musket—wild game.

As for Annis, all the evidence suggests that she was most certainly overworked and worn down by continual childbearing. The word *drudge* comes to mind. But in fostering such an image, I am using a twentieth-century perspective, being false to Annis and her times. In New England, the family was the labor pool. The South had its slaves, the mid-Atlantic states had indentured servants, New Englanders had children. A large family was viewed as an asset, and women perceived children in the light of a family-based economy. Having children was difficult, of course, but raising them was not the same task that it is today. Daughters were production assistants, an absolute necessity in the home. Sons were needed as working partners for their fathers. An equal mixture of both sexes was considered a gift of Providence.

What makes Annis unique in my eyes is that, in spite of her many duties and preoccupations, she managed to endow her daughters with the vision that they were something over and above the typical New England housewife. They grew up with the sense that they were ladies, that they must hold their backs straight, their heads high, and keep their skin magnolia white. Their mother's own personality and example provide the key here. In a state of isolation totally foreign to her upbringing in Massachusetts, the only solace for the romantic Annis was to conjure up visions of the past. While she spun and wove and rocked the baby, Annis told her daughters stories: stories she had heard from her mother about summers on the Rhode Island Sound— the sea, the gulls, and the marsh grasses; stories about growing up in a place where everyone was a cousin, where little girls wore fine white muslin, tucked and pleated into delicate gowns. Annis would have had such gowns as a child. Did she long for them, there in the wilderness?

How many times did she relate the family legend concerning their lofty ancestor, Pierre Grennelle, the Duke of Bourgogne, whose descendant Mathieu became a Huguenot and fled France for his life?

Adolphus, smoking a pipe in his homespun waistcoat and breeches, might have chided Annis gently for her fancies, amusing them instead with caustic descriptions of Tory gentlemen—the "macaronis" with their brocade waistcoats, velvet jackets, and jeweled buckles. Surely, to young girls, this was the stuff of which dreams were made.

Did Vira Ann lie awake nights under her homemade quilt exchanging whispered wishes with her older sister Permelia? Did they ever wish to glimpse the sea? To visit France? To wear satin? I think they did.

Another window on the larger world was school. In many places along the frontier, literacy was lost. But Annis saw that her large brood, even the girls, were educated. How did she manage an entire domestic economy—slaughtering, cooking, preserving, soap-making, laundering, spinning, weaving, sewing, candle-making, nursing—for such a large family if she let the girls go to school? No wonder Vira Ann always valued her education so highly!

Though Vira Ann surely had her Romantic streak, growing up in such confined circumstances acquainted her early with the realities of life. When she was not quite three years old, her mother endured another childbirth and Cordelia was born. During the next fourteen years there would be eight more births. Annis was attended by a local midwife, with Dr. Archibald Farr (who also ran the local tavern) available for emergencies. But in those days, bearing children was somewhat of a community happening. In the last stages of labor, "the women" would be called—Annis's neighbors. As Dr. Laurel Thatcher Ulrich relates in her biography of a New England midwife, "Once the second stage of labor began . . . additional women were needed. Most early American women literally gave birth in the arms or on the laps of their neighbors. . . . The attending women offered emotional as well as physical support. . . . Performing their simple duties, they no doubt traded stories, measuring one woman's pains or the size of her child against another's."

Vira Ann was very aware of all that was entailed in giving birth. In her teenage years, she would have been one of the women in assistance, witnessing firsthand her mother's difficulty and attempts at stoicism. She would have helped to bind Annis up afterward with linen and soothing herbs, and wrap her in warming blankets to assuage her postpartum trembling. Tending the new infant was part of a daughter's job during the time referred to as a mother's "lying-in" before she "returned to her kitchen."

By the standards of that day, the Frenches were fortunate. Not one child was lost in childbirth, and only Judson died before he reached the age of one year. In their ratio of girls to boys, they weren't so lucky. There were only five boys to the ten girls, with two of the sons dying in childhood. This lack of sons was to make providing for his family more difficult for Adolphus as their numbers grew.

Did Vira Ann ever have the urge to climb the ridge that rose behind their cabin, to see what she could see? She was restless all of her life. I can see her wearing the obligatory sunbonnet, tying up her skirts, and risking a scolding for wearing out her precious shoe leather in an afternoon's truancy. What did she think when she reached the top of the ridge? Settling her skirts around her, she sat and contemplated her future. As far as her eye could see, the landscape was the same—lakes, rolling hills, and forest. There was no place for her dreams to happen. No elegant parlors, no seashore, no roomful of eligible beaux. The outside world was limited to what she could see now, and the dry, outdated words of her father's newspaper that came by slow post.

But she was beautiful, and her mother had prepared her to be a lady. There was a whole world beyond the tiny village of Spafford. Would she ever see it?

Even her Romantically primed imagination couldn't have invented a life as extraordinary and rich as the one she was to lead. But before she arrived at that time, Vira Ann had to leave childhood behind and struggle through the lonely valley of loss.

The bulk of the farm in Spafford was sold after only two years, for eight hundred dollars. Adolphus had made a tidy profit on his investment, but the sale left him with only sixteen acres of land, presumably just enough for a house, a milk cow, some chickens, a vegetable garden, and a fruit orchard. How did he provide for his family? The 1820 census lists his profession as agriculture. The land was better suited for fruit farming than grain, so perhaps Adolphus decided to make the switch, selling the rest of his land at nearly double the price he paid for it.

As it turned out, his decision was a wise one. With the opening of the Erie Canal in 1825, cheap western wheat was available in quantities and at prices with which the Onondaga farmers and their tiny acreages could not compete. The value of land fell as low as $10.00 per acre, half the price Adolphus had received for his land in 1818. After the opening of the canal, life took a grim turn for the farmers in Onondaga. No longer able to earn enough means to support his still-growing family, Adolphus joined with many of his neighbors, migrating west along the Great Genessee Road to find work in Orleans County, New York, where new opportunities had blossomed with the opening of the canal. The rest of the family stayed behind.

The first summer he was gone, they suffered a difficult loss. Baby Judson died at the age of eight months. Perhaps their grief was assuaged slightly when Adolphus was home long enough to sire another child. In June of 1830, when Vira Ann was seventeen and Annis forty-one, this last baby, Amanda, was born. Six weeks after Amanda's birthday, the 1830 census was taken, showing Adolphus in Orleans with thirteen-year-old Enos. Adolphus, Jr., seems to have vanished, perhaps to Canada. Twenty-two-year-old Ethan was making his way west. The eldest daughter, Almira, was twenty-four and certainly married. New baby at her breast, Annis struggled together with her remaining daughters, striving to do the household work and the men's work besides.

Under these difficult circumstances, her robust health began to give way. The following year proved to be more than Annis could bear. First, her youngest son Lorenzo died in February, at the age of five years. Six months later, they lost Laura, age twenty-one. As autumn deepened into winter, Adolphus and Annis came to a decision to move the family west without waiting for spring. Why they decided to attempt such a desperate thing is not clear. Winters were harsh in upstate New York.

But misfortune had dogged them for four years. Things did not seem likely to get better in New York. Ethan wrote of new opportunities and cheap land in Michigan Territory. Perhaps they had experienced all they could stand, and gambled on another move west to put things right. After all, they could stick to the waterways, avoiding an overland trek. As long as the canals didn't freeze, travel wouldn't be difficult, winter notwithstanding. Whatever his reasoning, the decision to leave in December was one Adolphus would deeply regret.

Leaving behind all that was familiar, Annis and Adolphus, Permelia (19), Vira Ann (18), Cordelia (15), Enos (14), Wealthy (13), Mary (11), Sophia (9), Louvisa (7), and the baby Amanda boarded the packet boat that carried them down the Erie Canal to Buffalo, where they then climbed aboard a noisy steamboat for the five-day voyage across Lake Erie to Detroit in Michigan Territory.

The weather was bitter, and Annis proved too weak for the journey.

She died suddenly aboard ship. In a grim ceremony that haunted Vira Ann all her life, they buried her mother in the icy depths of Lake Erie.

She was given little time to mourn, for she and Permelia had to take immediate charge of Amanda, age eighteen months, as well as Louvisa and Sophia. How traumatic for the little ones to see their mother disappear inexplicably into the dark, menacing waters. And then to leave her! What a bleak, inconsolable time that must have been, traveling across the vast expanse of water, shrouded in freezing fog, pursued by Arctic winds and warm memories of a life that would never be again. Now what might have proved to be the exciting adventure Vira Ann had looked for was turned into a horrible nightmare.

Thus depleted and grief-stricken, the family arrived in Michigan. The heart seems to have gone out of Adolphus. There is very little record of him in the new territory. Ethan took charge of the family.

A carpenter by trade, Ethan knew his skills would be much in demand in the rough new settlements of western Michigan. Government land, purchased from the Potawatomi Indians, was selling for a dollar an acre. These two circumstances made the Kalamazoo River valley an ideal place for the Frenches to begin again.

As they took their journey over the Washtenaw Trail from Detroit, they saw a country very different from the New York wilderness. Southern Michigan was flat, covered with soggy marshes and streams.

The new town of Kalamazoo, or Bronson as it was then called, was built on steep bluffs that overlooked the river flatland where the lazy Kalamazoo River was joined by Arcadia and Portage creeks.

What did Vira Ann think of this new place? It would have been difficult for her to feel anything but discouragement initially. While Ethan, Adolphus, and Enos inspected land, looking for a place to farm, the family stayed in the Kalamazoo House hotel. Built partly of logs and partly of lumber hauled from the new mill in the next settlement, it was a thirty-by-forty, two-story building furnished with rough-hewn benches. After such a long, discouraging journey, Kalamazoo House did not provide much comfort. Settling the baby and her smaller sisters in their cramped accommodations, Vira Ann and Permelia knew they would have months of such living before they could finally settle in a home of their own.

The arrival of a family replete with daughters was a noteworthy event in Kalamazoo, however. Young settlers from the east had ridden out alone to seek their fortune and were eager for the company of young women. Rough and uncomfortable it certainly was, but Permelia and Vira Ann did not lack for admirers. Unlike the isolated village of Spafford, Kalamazoo was full of young, vital personalities.

Frontier hospitality was warm and welcoming, and the enthusiasm of their new neighbors was hard to resist. Undoubtedly, the Frenches were taken in by more established settlers, who were accustomed to inviting newcomers into their rough lodgings until they could build accommodations of their own. After their homogeneous Puritan community, Vira Ann and Permelia were struck by the variety in their new hometown. A contemporary historian described it as "a motley crew of Yankees, Hoosiers, Canuks, speculators, dogs, and Indians—the latter greatly predominating."

I can picture Vira Ann, still mourning her mother, looking around her at the foreign landscape, overwhelmed by her new responsibilities, and yet feeling her blood stir at the possibilities of this new place. There was opportunity here. Anything might happen.

Ethan finally decided on a forty-acre farm at the edge of the township, and putting his carpentry skills to work, he fashioned their first Michigan home. Thriving on the healthy frontier economy, he had plenty of work, and began courting the sister of Marcus Hounsom, owner of the local sawmill and one of the township's more enterprising citizens.

With Ethan in such demand, it was left to Adolphus and Enos to run the farm, and the daughters settled down to care for the family. Trying to keep the standards their mother had set was difficult in the new, raw community, but nevertheless, Vira Ann and Permelia took their responsibilities to heart.

Though they were far from civilization as they had known it, the Kalamazoo stores were filling with a wild assortment of merchandise. Eastern merchants, moved by the spirit of speculation, were eager to outfit the community. President Jackson had closed the federal bank, and the state banks were issuing their own inflated currency. Supply and demand determined the value of everything in Kalamazoo. The most curious items, such as fashion combs for the hair, might be had for next to nothing, while the price for a bushel of apples might equal the price of an acre of government land. Domestically manufactured cloth freed the French girls from their loom. Other things they might buy at local stores with Ethan's wages or in trade for wheat or corn from the farm were suspender buttons, pins, ribbon, thimbles, scissors, bonnets, parasols, brass fire tongs, lace caps, and even an opera cape!

Breaking the virgin ground was hard work, and Adolphus needed his ax to open holes for planting in the heavy prairie sod. Not yet broken to the plow, the ground was knotted in a tough underground root system. Eventually, they had to hire a giant "breaking plow" pulled by long lines of oxen to turn over the soil.

But the land was rich, far richer than their New York farm. Both wheat and corn grew well. Romance also flourished in the new territory, and by the end of 1832, Vira Ann's brother was in a position to propose to Matilda Hounsom. In the first marriage performed in Kalamazoo County, Matilda and Ethan were married on January 1, 1833, by Cyrus Lovell, justice of the peace.

This marriage was recorded by the newly appointed county clerk, Stephen Vickery, a handsome, well-educated young man who had come to the county in 1831 serving as schoolteacher and surveyor. With earnings from these two professions, he began investing in land in 1832 and courted the beautiful Permelia French, Vira Ann's older sister. He saw her as the perfect asset to his career (which would include several sessions in the state legislature and even the Whig nomination for governor).

Anthony Cooley, artist and early resident of the county, recorded in oils the first court held in Kalamazoo. Seated beneath the judge's bench, taking down the proceedings with his quill pen, is Stephen Vickery. The jurors, seated to his left, include Vira Ann's future father-in-law, Thomas Barber.

Vira Ann's suitor, Jonas Barber, was an entirely different man from the smooth, educated Stephen Vickery. Jonas embodied the entrepreneurial optimism and sweeping charisma of the successful frontiersman. There was nothing Jonas wasn't willing to try. Coming to Kalamazoo in 1830 with his father and family of brothers, he immediately purchased land in Prairie Ronde, a fertile area south of the town of Bronson. Raised in the harsh wilderness of northwest Pennsylvania, he was eager to test himself against the fertile Michigan prairie. By the time he met and courted Vira Ann, he was a man of some substance, independent from his father, full of ideas for the future.

With her wide choice of eligible young men, it says much about Vira Ann's character that she fell in love with Jonas Barber. In 1833 she was only twenty, but the sorrows and losses of the last five years had caused her to mature quickly and learn to rely on her own experience. Ultimately, her father had been unsuccessful in his frontier experiment. Choosing to cross Lake Erie in December was his crowning folly, costing her mother's life. An obedient daughter she probably was, but that didn't stop her from making silent judgments in her heart. If she must live on the frontier, she would marry someone equipped to handle the life.

Permelia chose a fellow New Yorker with a cultural background similar to her own. Vira Ann struck out into new territory. She chose providently, for Jonas was unusually well set up for a young man, but she also chose adventurously. Despite her need for security, Vira Ann had another, perhaps equal need for possibilities and change. Life would never be dull with Jonas Barber.

In 1834, Permelia married, leaving the family in Vira Ann's hands. While she acted as sole "mother" to the remaining French brood, Jonas continued to prosper, building the first sawmill in neighboring Van Buren County at Paw Paw. Milling was a lucrative industry on the frontier, as the first order of business was to clear the land and build. In a short time, he had a profitable concern.

Permelia had been married a year and was expecting her first child when Vira Ann and Jonas were finally married on November 1, 1835.

Settling down in her own house with her own husband, Vira Ann knew a sense of security that her life had lacked for many years. Jonas thought of her as a hard-won prize and was a generous husband.

She was allowed just eighteen days of peace before tragedy struck again. Permelia, companion of all her trials, died in childbirth, most probably in Vira Ann's arms.

Stephen was deeply grieved, Vira Ann nearly inconsolable. Permelia had been her dearest friend. They had dreamed together as children and then struggled together to overcome the odds against them in this new land. How could she be taken like this? Vira Ann's new sense of security quickly proved hollow.

Worst of all, she had to work out her anger and grief with the knowledge that she, too, was pregnant. Was Permelia's death due to negligence, to the absence of an experienced midwife? It is possible. What fears Vira Ann must have felt during the nine months of her own pregnancy.

There were other things to worry them, too. The land rush was at its peak, bringing with it a rash of speculators. A historian describes the scene: "It is probable that the year 1836 witnessed as great an amount of speculation in all parts of the country . . . as any year in the history of the republic. This spirit of speculation was manifested in the newer regions of the Union to a most remarkable degree. . . . Kalamazoo was continually filled with men looking for land and speculators watching for the unwary. A quarter section would sometimes be sold in the morning for two hundred dollars, which before night would again be sold for double that sum. Everybody was frantic to get hold of land, and men seemed to think that there was untold wealth in crazy speculation. . . . It is said that the sales for May, 1836, reach a half-million dollars."

In the summer of 1836, Andrew Jackson responded to this unruly fever by enacting the "Specie Circular," which provided that the government would only accept silver and gold in payment for land. Prior to this edict, speculator's notes and the dubious paper issued by unregulated "wildcat banks" had supported most of the land rush. The effect of Jackson's decree was to send the speculators home with their tails between their legs, leaving many unlucky settlers with lands bought at inflated prices, for which they could no longer even afford the taxes. These people left Kalamazoo, as well, allowing their property to be sold at sheriff's sales, just to cover taxes. The whole frontier was plunged into a depression that lasted for years.

What effect did this have on Jonas and Vira Ann? Jonas had purchased his lands in 1830 and 1831, before their value was inflated, so he escaped the plight of those who could not pay their taxes. It is probable, however, that his mill business suffered. The demand for lumber for new homes diminished greatly. Payment, when it came, was usually in "kind." Barter became the new economic system. For a lumber delivery, Jonas might receive a barrel of flour. Not needing this (his father-in-law raised wheat; his brother had a flour mill), he would take it into the store and use it to purchase cloth for Vira Ann and other manufactured goods that were heavy on the merchants' hands.

Jonas was able to weather the bad times and come out with his skin intact. But he could see which way the wind was blowing. Kalamazoo had fallen on hard times. It was no longer a place for a frontier entrepreneur.

He and his wife considered the situation. A new territory was opening for settlement in Iowa. On the other hand, their first child was due in September. After Permelia's death, could Jonas take his wife into another wilderness situation to give birth among strangers in the most primitive of conditions? He could, and he did. His own mother had borne a large family of children in uncomfortable circumstances. Would he expect his wife to be any different?

Why did Vira Ann choose to go with him, instead of staying behind with her family and joining him later? Surely she felt at risk! This battle between her need for security, her sense of duty, and her desire for adventure would be a constant in her life. Sometimes security won, but this time duty and adventure seemed to lie together. Heavily pregnant, Vira Ann went west to Iowa.

In the roughest of cabins along the Mississippi, attended by her younger sisters, she gave birth to her first son, Charles Edwin Barber, on the twenty-eighth day of September, 1836. In doing so, she triumphed over her fear. She had given birth and survived. And not only had she survived, she had brought a new human being into the world. A wonderful, miraculous, black-haired baby boy.

Charles at her breast, Vira Ann returned to the business of taming her husband and making a home.

Vira Ann and Jonas conquered many more frontiers together, ever westward. She made three round-trips across the plains, once at the head of thirty teams and wagons that carried all her worldly possessions from Illinois to Colorado. For years she had resisted the move. It was only when Charles returned safely from the Civil War and she wished to keep her other sons from joining up that she saw the obvious advantage of removing her family to join Jonas in the mountain gold camps of Colorado.

Her husband grew to be an extremely wealthy man, and tales of him as a founder of Princeton, Iowa; Rapids City, Illinois; and Golden, Colorado; have grown into legend. After two years in the gold camps of California, he returned to Illinois by sailing "round the horn" and up the Mississippi. Jonas and Vira Ann owned a piece of the Comstock Lode in Colorado, and interest in several gold mines.

In spite of the fact that he had three sons living, he left all he had to his wife upon his death. She never lost her air of superior gentility, and lived long enough to be a sore trial to her daughters-in-law, of whom she expected the same high standards she had kept throughout her life.

Though I only found this third great-grandmother of mine in my forties, knowledge of her life has affected me profoundly. Despite the vast difference in our times and circumstances, the central conflict of our lives is the same.

It should be clear to any reader that surviving her environment was the overriding theme of Vira Ann's life. Though often temporarily defeated by her circumstances, in the end she succeeded in passing on to her posterity her unique gifts and vision, having clung to them in spite of all the onslaughts that pioneer life made upon her.

I have not lived on the physical frontier, but rather a kind of spiritual/emotional frontier. Entering adulthood in the sixties, my generation and I experienced the wholesale betrayal of our trust by our government as thousands of our age died in a senseless war that was fed by lies and misplaced patriotism. In horror and confusion, we realized that our government was not only *not our protector, but our predator*. Like some vast dysfunctional family, we tried to deal with this betrayal. Many turned to drugs as a way out of a spiritual vacuum, becoming entangled in the web of crime and moral corruption that has plagued the country ever since.

Whom could we trust? Whom could we believe? Every value we were taught became suspect.

After Vietnam, Watergate, and the turmoil of the civil rights movement, we did not emerge with many illusions. "Never trust anyone over thirty" was a credo implicit in our world view. Hence, the feeling of having to start over, to build from scratch. In time, of course, we realized that we were not the first to experience this type of disillusionment.

As in times past, many of us have simply given up, subscribing to hedonism as the only god of this world. Others have gone on one spiritual search after another, from Zen to fundamentalism, seeking an anchor, seeking passionately for something to believe in. Some, like me, have even become reverse pioneers—forsaking urban life and values in search of Thoreau's simplicity and peace in rural America.

In my struggle with my environment, I want to share with Vira Ann the same determination not to give in or give up, but to keep on going. I know that like her, I am a "reins-grabber." In other words, if nothing is happening, I make something happen. This is, of course, not always a comfortable policy, but I have learned that it is certainly in the genes.

Consider the evidence. My ninth great-grandfather, Mathieu Grinnell, forsook a life of aristocratic ease because he could not in good conscience remain a Catholic. Because of their beliefs, others of my foreparents—Thomas Rogers, James Chilton, Mary Chilton, and Richard Warren—turned their backs on their native land, venturing forth into the unknown on a tiny vessel called the *Mayflower*. Mary is especially close to my heart. As a twelve-year-old girl, she could not restrain her excitement and left the ship while the other women were still awaiting a time when the men might consider it safe for them to do so. Hitching up her skirts, Mary ran barefoot through the tide, anxious to set her feet on the New World, to embrace the experiences ahead of her.

Descendants of Mary left Plymouth for Rhode Island in protest against the autocratic ways of the Pilgrim fathers. Their descendants made another break, fighting England in a war for independence and then striking out to foster new settlements and new values in the West. The children of this generation moved further west, building commerce and industry as they went, finding wealth and prosperity as America became a world power. It was into that world that I was born.

Is it surprising that what was of vital interest to my forebears should be of interest to me? Is it surprising that I should consider breaking with the past, sailing into the unknown, my precious values in a pack upon my back? My ancestors, Vira Ann included, were certainly not perfect, but they had one thing in common: they were all hopeful survivors. *My knowledge of their struggles to overcome the ills of their world, to make it a better place for their children, helps me in a very real way to do the same.*

In Act III of *Our Town* the Stage Manager makes the following observation: "Now there are some things we all know, but we don't take'm out and look at'm very often. We all know that *something* is eternal. And it ain't houses and it ain't names, and it ain't earth, and it ain't even the stars . . . everybody knows in their bones that *something* is eternal, and that something has to do with human beings. All the greatest people ever lived have been telling us that for five thousand years and you'd be surprised how people are always losing hold of it. There's something way down deep that's eternal about every human being."

What is eternal about Vira Ann and my other ancestors speaks to that which is eternal in me. The message is love and hope. With that I am warmed, embraced, and empowered to go on.

APPENDIX A

Where to Write for Vital Records

Alabama

Birth, death, marriage, divorce: Center for Health Statistics, State Department of Public Health, 434 Monroe Street, Montgomery, AL 36130. Since January 1908. No personal checks. (205) 242-5033 to verify current fees.

Alaska

Birth, death, marriage, divorce: Department of Health and Social Services, Bureau of Vital Statistics, P.O. Box H-02G, Juneau, AK 99811-0675. Since January 1913. No personal checks. (907) 465-3391 to verify current fees.

Arizona

Birth, death: Vital Records Section of Arizona Department of Health Services, P.O. Box 3887, Phoenix, AZ 85030. Since July 1909. Check or money order. Applicants must submit a copy of picture identification or have their request notarized. (602) 542-1080 to verify current fees. *Marriage, divorce:* Clerk of Superior Court in county where license or divorce was granted.

Arkansas

Birth, death, marriage, divorce: Division of Vital Records, Arkansas Department of Health, 4815 West Markham Street, Little Rock, AR 72201. Since February 1914. Check or money order. (501) 661-2336 to verify current fees.

California

Birth, death, marriage, divorce: Vital Statistics Section, Department of Health Services, 410 N Street, Sacramento, CA 95814. Since July 1905. Check or money order payable to State Registrar, Department of Health Services. (916) 445-2684 to verify current fees.

Colorado

Birth, death, marriage, divorce: Vital Records Section, Colorado Department of Health, 4210 East 11th Avenue, Denver, CO 80220. Death, marriage, divorce records since 1900. Birth records since 1910. Check or money order. (303) 320-8474 to verify current fees.

Connecticut

Birth, death, marriage: Vital Records, Department of Health Services, 150 Washington Street, Hartford, CT 06101. Since July 1897. Check or money order. (203) 566-2334 to verify current fees. *Divorce:* Index of records since 1947. Contact clerk of superior court where divorce was granted.

Delaware

Birth, death, marriage, divorce: Office of Vital Statistics, Division of Public Health, P.O. Box 637, Dover, DE 19903. Death records since 1930, birth since 1920, marriage since 1930, divorce since 1935. Check or money order. (302) 736-4721 to verify current fees.

District of Columbia

Birth, death: Vital Records Branch, Room 3009, 435 I Street, Washington, DC 20001. Death records since 1855 (except during Civil War), birth records since 1874. Cashier's check or money order to D.C. treasurer. (202) 727-9281 to verify current fees. *Marriage:* Clerk, Superior Court for the District of Columbia, Family Division, 500 Indiana Avenue NW, Washington, DC 20001. Records since September 16, 1956. Fee $2.00. *Divorce:* Clerk, U.S. District Court for the District of Columbia, Washington, DC 20001. Records since September 16, 1956.

Florida

Birth, death, marriage, divorce: Department of Health and Rehabilitative Services, Office of Vital Statistics, 1217 Pearl Street, Jacksonville, FL 32202. Some birth back to April 1865, some death back to August 1877. Most records from January 1917. Marriage and divorce since June 6, 1927. Check or money order. (904) 359-6900 to verify current fees.

Georgia

Birth, death, marriage: Georgia Department of Human Resources, Vital Records Unit, Room 217-H, 47 Trinity Avenue SW, Atlanta, GA

30334. Records since January 1919. Money order only, payable to Vital Records, Ga. DHR. (404) 656–4900 to verify current fees. *Divorce:* Clerk of superior court in county where divorce was granted. Records since June 9, 1952, only.

Hawaii
Birth, death, marriage, divorce: Office of Health Status Monitoring, State Department of Health, P.O. Box 3378, Honolulu, HI 96801. Records since 1853. Check or money order. (808) 548–5819 to verify current fees.

Idaho
Birth, death, marriage, divorce: Vital Statistics Unit, Idaho Department of Health and Welfare, 450 West State Street, Statehouse Mail, Boise, ID 83720–9990. Has records since 1911. Check or money order. (208) 334–5988 to verify current fees.

Illinois
Birth, death, marriage, divorce: Division of Vital Records, Illinois Department of Public Health, 605 West Jefferson St., Springfield, IL 62072–5079. Records since January 1916. Money order or check. (217) 782–6653 to verify current fees.

Indiana
Birth, death, marriage: Vital Records Section, State Board of Health, 1330 West Michigan Street, P.O. Box 1964, Indianapolis, IN 46206–1964. Birth records since October 1907, death records since 1900, marriage index since 1958. (317) 633–0274 to verify current fees. *Divorce:* County Clerk where divorce was issued.

Iowa
Birth, death, marriage, divorce: Iowa Department of Public Health, Vital Records Section, Lucas Office Building, 321 East 12th Street, Des Moines, IA 50319. Records since July 1880. Check or money order. (515) 281–5871 to verify current fees.

Kansas
Birth, death, marriage, divorce: Office of Vital Statistics, Kansas State Department of Health and Environment, 900 Jackson Street, Topeka, KS 66612–1290. Birth and death records since July 1911, marriage

records since May 1913, divorce records since 1951. Check or money order. (913) 296-1400 to verify current fees.

Kentucky

Birth, death, marriage, divorce: Office of Vital Statistics, Department for Health Services, 275 East Main Street, Frankfort, KY 40621. Birth and death records since 1911, marriage and divorce records since June 1958. Check or money order. (502) 564-4212 to verify current fees.

Louisiana

Birth, death, marriage: Vital Records Registry, Office of Public Health, 325 Loyola Avenue, New Orleans, LA 70112. State has records since July 1914. (504) 568-2561 to verify current fees. City of New Orleans has births from 1790 and deaths from 1803. Check or money order. *Divorce:* Clerk of court in parish where license was granted.

Maine

Birth, death, marriage, divorce: Office of Vital Records, Human Services Building, Station 11, State House, Augusta, ME 04333. State has records since 1892. Check or money order. (207) 289-3184 to verify current fees.

Maryland

Birth, death, marriage, divorce: Division of Vital Records, Department of Health and Mental Hygiene, Metro Executive Building, 4201 Patterson Avenue, P.O. Box 68760, Baltimore, MD 21215-0020. Birth and death records since August 1898, marriage records since June 1951, divorce records since January 1961. Check or money order. (301) 225-5988 to verify current fees. Records for city of Baltimore since January 1875. Will not do research for genealogical studies. Must apply to State of Maryland Archives, 350 Rowe Boulevard, Annapolis, MD 21401; (301) 974-3914.

Massachusetts

Birth, death, marriage, divorce: Registry of Vital Records and Statistics, 150 Tremont Street, Room B-3, Boston, MA 02111. Records since 1896. Check or money order payable to Commonwealth of Massachusetts. (617) 727-7388 to verify current fees. For earlier records, write to the Massachusetts Archives at Columbia Point, 220 Morrissey Boulevard, Boston, MA 02125; (617) 727-2816.

Michigan
Birth, death, marriage, divorce: Office of the State Registrar and Center for Health Statistics, Michigan Department of Public Health, 3423 North Logan Street, Lansing, MI 48909. Records since 1867. Check or money order. (517) 335-8655 to verify current fees.

Minnesota
Birth, death, marriage, divorce: Minnesota Department of Health, Section of Vital Statistics, 717 Delaware Street SE, P.O. Box 9441, Minneapolis, MN 55440. Records since 1908. Check or money order to Treasurer, State of Minnesota. (612) 623-5121 to verify current fees.

Mississippi
Birth, death, marriage, divorce: Vital Records, State Department of Health, 2423 North State Street, Jackson, MS 39216. Has records since 1912. Accepts only bank or postal money orders. (601) 960-7981 to verify current fees.

Missouri
Birth, death, marriage, divorce: Department of Health, Bureau of Vital Records, 1730 E. Elm, P.O. Box 570, Jefferson City, MO 65102. Has records since 1910. Check or money order. (314) 751-6376 to verify current fees. Marriage and divorce indexes since July 1948.

Montana
Birth, death, marriage, divorce: Bureau of Records and Statistics, State Department of Health and Environmental Sciences, Helena, MT 59620. Has records since 1907. Check or money order. (406) 444-2614 to verify current fees. Marriage and divorce records since 1943.

Nebraska
Birth, death, marriage, divorce: Bureau of Vital Statistics, State Department of Health, 301 Centennial Mall South, P.O. Box 95007, Lincoln, NE 68509-5007. Has birth, death records since late 1904, marriage and divorce records since January 1909. Check or money order. (402) 471-2871 to verify current fees.

Nevada
Birth, death, marriage, divorce: Division of Health—Vital Statistics, Capitol Complex, 505 East King Street #102, Carson City, NV 89710.

Has birth and death records since July 1911, marriage and divorce indexes since January 1968. Check or money order. (702) 885-4480 to verify current fees.

New Hampshire
Birth, death, marriage, divorce: Bureau of Vital Records, Health and Human Services Building, 6 Hazen Drive, Concord, NH 03301. Has birth, marriage, death records since 1640, divorce records since 1808. (603) 271-4654 to verify current fees.

New Jersey
Birth, death, marriage: State Department of Health, Bureau of Vital Statistics, South Warren and Market Streets, CN 370, Trenton, NJ 08625 (for records from June 1878). Archives and History Bureau, State Library Division, State Department of Education, Trenton, NJ 08625 (for records from May 1848 to May 1878). Check or money order. (609) 292-4087 to verify current fees. *Divorce:* Superior Court, Chancery Division, State House Annex, CN 971, Trenton, NJ 08625. Two dollars for first four pages. Additional pages at fifty cents each.

New Mexico
Birth, death: Vital Statistics, New Mexico Health Services Division, 1190 St. Francis Drive, Santa Fe, NM 87503. Records since 1920 and delayed records since 1880. Check or money order. (505) 827-2338 to verify current fees. *Marriage:* County clerk in county where license was issued. *Divorce:* Clerk of superior court where divorce was granted.

New York
Birth, death, marriage, divorce: Vital Records Section, State Department of Health, Empire State Plaza, Tower Building, Albany, NY 12237-0023. Has birth, death, and marriage records since 1880. For records before 1914 in Albany, Buffalo, and Yonkers, or before 1880 in any other city, write to registrar of vital statistics in city where event occurred. For the rest of the state, except New York City, write to the state office. Check or money order. (518) 474-3075 to verify current fees. For marriage records from 1880 to 1907 and licenses issued in the cities of Albany, Buffalo, or Yonkers, apply to: Albany—City Clerk, City Hall, Albany, NY 12207; Buffalo—City Clerk, City Hall, Buf-

falo, NY 14202; Yonkers—Registrar of Vital Statistics, Health Center Building, Yonkers, NY 10701.

New York City

Birth, death: Bureau of Vital Records, Department of Health of New York City, 125 Worth Street, New York, NY 10013. Birth records since 1898 and death records since 1930. For Old City of New York (Manhattan and part of Bronx) birth records for 1865–97 and death records for 1865–1929, write to Archives Division, Department of Records and Information Services, 31 Chambers Street, New York, NY 10007. Money order only. (212) 619–4530 to verify current fees. *Marriage:* Bronx Borough—City Clerk's Office, 1780 Grand Concourse, Bronx, NY 10457. Brooklyn Borough—City Clerk's Office, Municipal Building, Brooklyn, NY 11201. Manhattan Borough—City Clerk's Office, Municipal Building, New York, NY 10007. Queens Borough—City Clerk's Office, 120-55 Queens Boulevard, Kew Gardens, NY 11424. Staten Island Borough—City Clerk's Office, Staten Island Borough Hall, Staten Island, NY 10301. Records from 1847 to 1865. For records from 1866 to 1907, write Archives Division, Department of Records and Information Services, 31 Chambers Street, New York, NY 10007 (except Brooklyn records, which are filed with County Clerk's Office, Kings County, Supreme Court Building, Brooklyn, NY 11201). *Divorce:* See New York State.

North Carolina

Birth, death, marriage, divorce: Department of Environment, Health, and Natural Resources, Division of Epidemiology, Vital Records Section, 225 North McDowell Street, P.O. Box 27687, Raleigh, NC 27611–7687. Birth records since October 1913, death records since January 1930. Death records from 1913 to 1929 available from Archives and Records Section, State Records Center, 215 North Blount Street, Raleigh, NC 27602. Marriage records since 1962, divorce records since 1958. Check or money order. (919) 733-3526 to verify current fees.

North Dakota

Birth, death, marriage, divorce: Division of Vital Records, State Capitol, 600 East Boulevard Avenue, Bismarck, ND 58505. Has some birth and death records since July 1893. 1894–1920 incomplete. Marriage records since July 1925, index of divorce records since July 1949. Money order. (701) 224-2360 to verify current fees.

Ohio

Birth, death, marriage, divorce: Division of Vital Statistics, Ohio Department of Health, G-20 Ohio Department Building, 65 South Front Street, Columbus, OH 43266-0333. Has birth records since December 20, 1908. For earlier birth and death records, write to the probate court in county where event occurred. Marriage and divorce records since September 1949. Check or money order. (614) 466-2531 to verify fees.

Oklahoma

Birth, death: Vital Records Section, State Department of Health, 1000 Northeast 10th Street, P.O. Box 53551, Oklahoma City, OK 73152. Has records since 1908. Check or money order. (405) 271-4040 to verify current fees. *Marriage, divorce:* Clerk of court in county where event took place.

Oregon

Birth, death, marriage, divorce: Oregon Health Division, Vital Statistics Section, P.O. Box 116, Portland, OR 97207. Has birth and death records since January 1903, marriage records since January 1906, divorce records since 1925. Check or money order. (503) 229-5710 to verify current fees.

Pennsylvania

Birth, death, marriage, divorce: Division of Vital Records, State Department of Health, Central Building, 101 South Mercer Street, P.O. Box 1528, New Castle, PA 16103. State has records since January 1906, except for divorce, which begin in January 1946. Check or money order. (412) 656-3147 to verify current fees.

Rhode Island

Birth, death, marriage: Division of Vital Records, Rhode Island Department of Health, Room 101, Cannon Building, 3 Capitol Hill, Providence, RI 02908-5097. Has records since 1853. Money order to General Treasurer, State of Rhode Island. (401) 277-2811 to verify current fees. *Divorce:* Clerk of Family Court, Dorrance Plaza, Providence, RI 02903.

South Carolina

Birth, death, marriage, divorce: Office of Vital Records and Public Health Statistics, South Carolina Department of Health and Environmental Control, 2600 Bull Street, Columbia, SC 29201. Has birth and death records since January 1915, marriage records since July 1950, divorce records since April 1949. Check or money order. (803) 734-4830 to verify current fees.

South Dakota

Birth, death, marriage, divorce: State Department of Health, Center for Health Policy and Statistics, Vital Records, 523 East Capitol, Pierre, SD 57501. State office has records since July 1905 and access to other records for some events that occurred before then. Money order or personal check. (605) 773-3355 to verify current fees.

Tennessee

Birth, death, marriage, divorce: Tennessee Vital Records, Department of Health and Environment, Cordell Hull Building, Nashville, TN 37219-5402. State office has birth records for state since January 1914, for Nashville since June 1881, for Knoxville since July 1881, and for Chattanooga since January 1882. Death records for state since January 1914, for Nashville since July 1874, for Knoxville since July 1887, and for Chattanooga since March 6, 1872. Marriage and divorce records since July 1945. Check or money order. (615) 741-1763 to verify current fees.

Texas

Birth, death, marriage, divorce: Bureau of Vital Statistics, Texas Department of Health, 1100 West 49th Street, Austin, TX 78756-3191. Birth and death records since 1903, marriage records since 1966, divorce records since January 1968. Check or money order. (512) 458-7451 to verify current fees.

Utah

Birth, death, marriage, divorce: Bureau of Vital Records, Utah Department of Health, 288 North 1460 West, P.O. Box 16700, Salt Lake City, UT 84116-0700. Birth and death records since 1905, marriage and divorce records since 1978. Check or money order. (801) 538-6105 to verify current fees.

Vermont

Birth, death, marriage, divorce (after 1955): Vermont Department of Health, Vital Records Section, Box 70, 60 Main Street, Burlington, VT 05402. Check or money order. (802) 863-7275 to verify current fees. *Birth, death, marriage (prior to 1955):* Division of Public Records, 6 Baldwin Street, Montpelier, VT 05602.

Virginia

Birth, death, marriage, divorce: Division of Vital Records, State Health Department, P.O. Box 1000, Richmond, VA 23208-1000. Has birth, death, and marriage records from January 1853 to December 1896 and since June 14, 1912. For records between those dates, write to city where event occurred. Divorce records since January 1918. Check or money order. (804) 786-6228 to verify current fees.

Washington

Birth, death, marriage, divorce: Vital Records, 1112 South Quince, P.O. Box 9709, ET-11, Olympia, WA 98504-9709. State office has birth and death records since July 1907, marriage and divorce records since 1968. Money order. (800) 331-0680 to verify current fees.

West Virginia

Birth, death, marriage, divorce: Vital Registration Office, Division of Health, State Capitol Complex Building 3, Charleston, WV 25305. Has birth and death records since January 1917, marriage records since 1921, divorce index since 1968. Check or money order. (304) 348-2931 to verify current fees.

Wisconsin

Birth, death, marriage, divorce: Vital Records, 1 West Wilson Street, P.O. Box 309, Madison, WI 53701. Scattered records before 1857. Records before October 1, 1907, incomplete. Check or money order. (608) 266-1371 to verify current fees.

Wyoming

Birth, death, marriage, divorce: Vital Records Service, Hathaway Building, Cheyenne, WY 82002. Birth and death records since 1909, marriage and divorce records since May 1941. Money order. (307) 777-7591 to verify current fees.

APPENDIX B

Four Family History Software Packages

There are many genealogy programs on the market today. Four of the most popular software packages will be discussed here. Each one is geared to different needs and interests, but there is one thing they all have in common: GEDCOM. GEDCOM is a utility that converts your data to a universal genealogy file, enabling you to send and receive data to and from different software programs.

The GEDCOM feature is essential in a software package if you wish to take advantage of the Ancestral File, which was discussed in Chapter Six. Ancestral File, available on CD-ROM at the Family History Centers of the Church of Jesus Christ of Latter-day Saints, gives you access to thousands of pedigrees submitted by other genealogists. By searching the index to the file you will probably find that at least one of your lines has already been researched by someone else. GEDCOM enables you to copy the desired pedigree, complete with names, dates, places, and family group sheets, directly onto a disk. When you get home, GEDCOM allows you to insert this pedigree into your own system, tying it into your own pedigree without typing in each individual name.

Everyone is encouraged to send his or her pedigree to the Ancestral File and become part of this vast store of information. The easiest way to do this is with a GEDCOM file. Specific details are given in Chapter Six.

GEDCOM also makes it easy for you to send and receive computerized information to and from other genealogists you correspond with, as well as family members who have computers. It is definitely a feature to consider when you are investing in software.

Which software package should you buy? Programs are written by different personalities—right-brained (the intuitive Sherlock Holmes type), left-brained (the structured, orderly Hercule Poirot type), and in between. Some programs are difficult to learn, some are very user-friendly. Your choice of software should be determined by your needs, your computer skill, and, of course, your pocketbook.

1. Personal Ancestral File (PAF)

For the beginner, PAF is a good choice. It is the most widely used genealogy program and it is also the least expensive. Produced and sold at cost by the Church of Jesus Christ of Latter-day Saints, it is priced at a mere thirty-five dollars, including shipping. It can be ordered by calling (801) 531–2584 or writing Salt Lake Distribution Center, 1999 West 1700 South, Salt Lake City, UT 84104. Versions are available for the Macintosh, Apple, IBM PC and its clones, and Kaypro.

I am not a computer genius by any means, and I find PAF extremely user-friendly. I was able to find my way around the program the first time I used it.

The following is a brief demonstration of how it works. Your first menu is shown in Illustration B.1. In order to begin your pedigree, you choose item 1, Add Records. The screen shown in Illustration B.2 will appear.

I always add families, even if I don't have all the members at the time. This automatically ties all the individuals together. Choose item 2. You will see the screen shown in Illustration B.3.

RIN refers to the number that is used to identify each individual in the data base. The computer automatically assigns this number and it becomes the computer's code for that person. It has no other significance. Since you are just beginning, the husband in your family is not in the file, so you choose option 1, which will bring up the template in Illustration B.4.

You simply type in your information, moving from field to field by using ENTER. When you have entered all your data, you press F1 to save and exit. The computer will ask you if you wish to create notes. If you say yes, a blank screen will appear. This is where you enter all your sources of information for this person. Notes preceded by an exclamation point will appear on printouts. Notes not so designated will only appear on the computer screen.

You will then enter the wife's information in a similar manner, and after pressing F1, the computer will give you a marriage template.

After completing this form, you will automatically be given the tem-

```
-------------------------
PERSONAL ANCESTRAL FILE
-------------------------
        MAIN MENU

1. Add Records
2. Modify Records
3. Delete Records
4. Pedigree Search
5. Notes
6. Print Forms and Reports
7. Focus/Design Reports
8. Match/Merge
9. Facts and Fun
A. Utilities
0. Return to System

Please enter your selection:
```

Illustration B.1

```
-------------------------
PERSONAL ANCESTRAL FILE
-------------------------
     ADD RECORDS MENU

    1. Add Individual
    2. Add Family
    0. Return to Main Menu

Please enter your selection:
```

Illustration B.2

```
        ----------
        ADD FAMILY
        ----------

       IDENTIFY HUSBAND

1. Husband not yet in file, add him
2. Husband in file--Know RIN
3. Husband in file--Do not Know RIN
4. Husband not known
0. Return to Previous Menu--DO NOT STORE FAMILY

       Please enter your selection:
```

Illustration B.3

plate for child number one and so on. When you have added all the children, you will have your first family.

Now, let's say you want to enter the husband's parents. You begin again from the main menu: Add records. Then: Add family. Everything proceeds exactly the same as in the first example, until you get to the "add child" menu shown in Illustration B.5.

When you wish to add the child who you have already entered as husband in the first family, you select either option number 2, if you know his RIN number, or option 3, if you don't. Option 3 will show a blank template in which you fill in the name of the person you want, and the computer will search until it finds him.

Once you have two generations on your pedigree, you can then switch to a less cumbersome way of entering families. Go back to the main menu and choose option 4, Pedigree Search. Your pedigree will appear before you. An example is shown in Illustration B.6.

```
                         INDIVIDUAL DATA                          (Husband)
-----------------------------------------------------------------------------
Sex:M      SURNAME:Vandagriff     Given1:David                      RIN:80
           Given2:P.              Given3:            Title:
-----------------------------------------------------------------------------
BIRTH          Date:25 Oct 1947
   PLACE   Level 1:Ames              Level 2:Story
           Level 3:Iowa              Level 4:
CHRISTENING Date:
   PLACE       L 1:                      L 2:
               L 3:                      L 4:
DEATH          Date:
   PLACE       L 1:                      L 2:
               L 3:                      L 4:
BURIAL         Date:
   PLACE       L 1:                      L 2:
               L 3:                      L 4:
-----------------------------------------------------------------------------


-----------------------------------------------------------------------------
                                              ID NO.:
-----------------------------------------------------------------------------

F1 SAVE CHANGES AND EXIT      F2 QUIT WITHOUT SAVING CHANGES
```

Illustration B.4

```
                            ----------
                            ADD FAMILY
                            ----------

                         IDENTIFY CHILD #1

          1. Child not yet in file, add child
          2. Child in file--Know RIN
          3. Child in file--Do not Know RIN
          4. No more children--STORE RECORD
          0. Return to Previous Menu--DO NOT STORE FAMILY

                 Please enter your selection:
```

Illustration B.5

Let's say you want to add another generation on the father's line. You simple push F for father and the computer will show you the pedigree of the next generation.

You then push F again and the computer will bleep and say: "There is no father entered. Add him now? (Y/N)." You push Y and the father's template will appear. In this way you can go ahead and add fathers, mothers, and children, and they will be connected automatically on the pedigree you see before you on the screen. You can also use this system to edit any individual on the pedigree by pushing E.

Those are the basics of PAF. What can it do for you? As shown in Chapter Three, it can print out your pedigrees and family group sheets. One option, the cascading pedigree, is a feature where you merely indi-

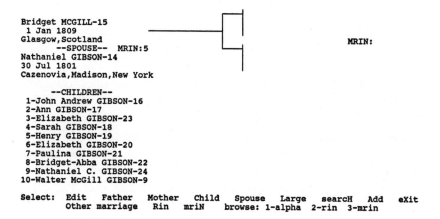

```
Bridget MCGILL-15
1 Jan 1809
Glasgow,Scotland                                        MRIN:
     --SPOUSE--   MRIN:5
Nathaniel GIBSON-14
30 Jul 1801
Cazenovia,Madison,New York

     --CHILDREN--
1-John Andrew GIBSON-16
2-Ann GIBSON-17
3-Elizabeth GIBSON-23
4-Sarah GIBSON-18
5-Henry GIBSON-19
6-Elizabeth GIBSON-20
7-Paulina GIBSON-21
8-Bridget-Abba GIBSON-22
9-Nathaniel C. GIBSON-24
10-Walter McGill GIBSON-9

Select:  Edit  Father  Mother  Child  Spouse  Large  searcH  Add  eXit
         Other marriage   Rin   mriN   browse: 1-alpha 2-rin 3-mrin
```

Illustration B.6

cate a person, and the computer prints out that person's entire pedigree, numbering pages and organizing them. My two-hundred-page pedigree took about two hours to print out on a dot matrix printer. A laser printer is much faster. Another option is the wall-size ancestry chart. Printed in strips that you tape together, this is a pedigree that shows you the big picture all at once. Mine covers all of the living room floor.

Another feature is sorted lists, which will sort your data according to whichever field you select (name, place, etc.) and print it out. Other lists identify specifics such as end-of-the-line individuals and surname frequencies.

A more interesting feature is the focus/design reports feature. This allows you to print reports that focus on particular things. For instance, if you were going to Michigan, you might like to print out a list of all your ancestors who died in Michigan. You could further narrow this down to a particular city or county.

Focused reports are designed by using a template on which you enter the information you wish to focus on. For instance, in the example mentioned above, you would first create a list focusing on Michigan as the place of death. The computer would then search for all individuals born in Michigan. After this, you would be shown how to create a report. Another option, if you are going to be searching chronological records, such as obituaries, would be to sort your list by date.

The items you can focus on are limited only by the field names, i.e., name, birthplace, birth date, burial place, etc. You can also sort according to any of these fields. For instance, I could have printed my death place list according to burial place. The computer would then have selected all individuals who died in Michigan and then arranged them so that all those buried in the same place were together. This would facilitate searching cemeteries. Producing these kinds of reports is one of the things that would be very difficult for you to do by hand that a computer will do very quickly. You can spend more time being a detective and less time shuffling papers.

A "facts and fun" menu offers a variety of features, including calculating relationships between any two people in your data base.

Compared to other programs, PAF is not fancy. It is not particularly sophisticated, but it works and it is very simple to use. The manual is excellent and easy to understand. I have found the telephone support system to be helpful when I have had a question. Don't be afraid to call if you need help.

If you decide you want to start with this program and then later decide to switch to another, you can use GEDCOM to painlessly and quickly convert your PAF data to the new data base, provided your new program supports GEDCOM.

II. *Everyone's Family Tree (EFT)*

This program, for IBM-compatible computers, is pure joy to use. It is so easy to learn that you scarcely need the manual. The help screens are very informative, and the menu available at each juncture is always shown at the bottom of the screen.

Unlike PAF, names are entered first as individuals rather than part of a family. Five templates appear during this process, one for name and sex, one for birth and christening information, one for death and burial information, one for last known residence, and finally one for notes. This screen can be used for typing in a small biography. Illustration B.7 shows the first template.

After the names have been added individually, they are linked using the pedigree screen shown in Illustration B.8. Moving the cursor to the desired spot on the pedigree, you merely press F5 to link individuals. In the case of a male ancestor, the computer will give you the surname and show a list of all the males in the name file with that

```
F1-Help          Everyone's Family Tree (tm)              File: MASTE
                    ┤ * * NAME FINDER * * ├
  Desc.
     SURNAME, Given                RIN #        Reference #

  ┌─ Page 1 ═════ INDIVIDUAL'S VITALS ═════
  │
  │            Surname: Vandagriff
  │         First Name: David
  │        Middle Name: Peter
  │    Additional Name:
  │                Sex: M      Desc. Report (+/ ):  +
  │              Title:
  │         Reference #:
  │
  └──────────────────────────────────────────────

   + │ , Barbara          │    829    │
   + │ , Beatrice         │   1014    │
   + │ , Beatrice         │   1060    │
   + │ , Begga            │   1093    │
   + │ , Bertha           │   1086    │
   +│  , de Thorndon      │   1018    │
```

David Peter Vandagriff

Illustration B.7

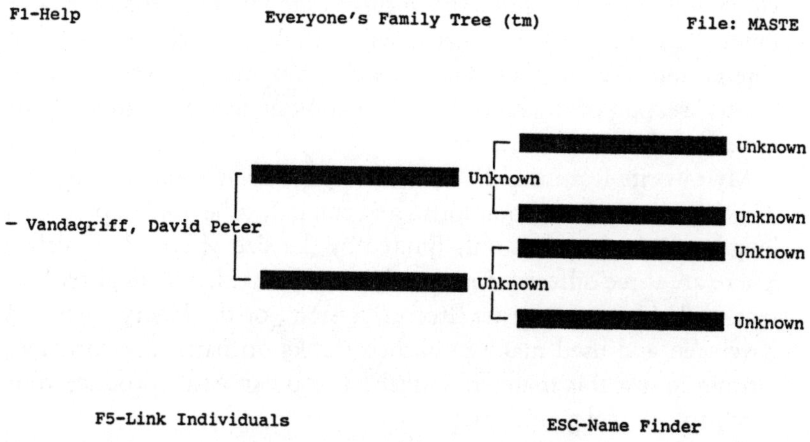

```
F1-Help          Everyone's Family Tree (tm)              File: MASTE
```

```
                                        ┌─ ████████████████ Unknown
                        ┌─ ████████████████ Unknown
                        │               └─ ████████████████ Unknown
   ─ Vandagriff, David Peter
                        │               ┌─ ████████████████ Unknown
                        └─ ████████████████ Unknown
                                        └─ ████████████████ Unknown
```

          F5-Link Individuals   ESC-Name Finder

Illustration B.8

surname. You move your cursor to the correct name and press ENTER. Your choice automatically appears at the desired place in the pedigree. When entering a female ancestor, you will be asked to provide the surname first.

Bill Dollarhide, creator of this program, prefers this method of entering individuals first and then tying them up later as the family relationships become known. With his system, the individuals will always appear on the alphabetized name-finder, and you can search for one in seconds using the FIND key. This means that even if you don't know how the individual fits into the scheme of things, you can still have his data in your master list. When you finally figure out where he fits, you can link him then.

Theoretically, this can be done in PAF as well. However, an individual not linked to a specific family in your pedigree could be easily forgotten, as there is no way that PAF can give you a list of all individuals in the data base unless you actually print out a list or take the time to have the computer do an alphabetical browse list (which takes forever!). Having your list of individual names constantly before you is one of the advantages of EFT over PAF.

Once you have entered and linked your names, you can print out several different reports that are really fun as well as professional looking. It can generate group sheets and pedigree charts, and also individual biographies or summary sheets as shown in Illustration B.9. A unique feature of EFT is that it will actually take the information entered into the templates and "write" a biography as shown in the "vitals" section of the report. Another unique feature is an ancestor table for a particular surname.

My favorite feature of EFT, however, is the Descendancy Report. This is printed out in book form, and can in fact be used to prepare a long book. Its length is only limited by the size of your hard drive. There are three different formats that can be used: The Register System, the Modified Register/Record System, or the Henry System. I have seen and used many published books on particular surnames written in just this manner. With EFT you can easily produce your own professional genealogy.

For documentation of your sources, there is a separate program called the Research Log. It follows Dollarhide's filing system. Illustration B.10 shows the template that is used to enter information. "Book" refers to the surname binder in which he advises you to keep all of your notes, stapled onto loose-leaf pages. Individuals are easily identified by their names and the RIN numbers, which appear in the Name Finder in your master file. The advantage to this is that your notations are concise and lead you directly to the place where you can find your documentation. The disadvantage is that if you do not decide to use Dollarhide's system, the Research Log won't do you much good. Also,

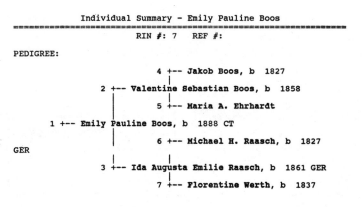

```
         Individual Summary - Emily Pauline Boos
========================================================================
                   RIN #: 7    REF #:

PEDIGREE:

                              4 +-- Jakob Boos, b  1827
                              |
                   2 +-- Valentine Sebastian Boos, b  1858
                   |          |
                   |          5 +-- Maria A. Ehrhardt
                   |
      1 +-- Emily Pauline Boos, b  1888 CT
                   |          6 +-- Michael H. Raasch, b  1827
      GER          |          |
                   |          |
                   3 +-- Ida Augusta Emilie Raasch, b  1861 GER
                              |
                              7 +-- Florentine Werth, b  1837
```

VITALS:

Emily Pauline Boos, daughter of Valentine Sebastian Boos and of Ida Augusta Emilie Raasch, born 25 Sep 1888 Hamden, New Haven, Connecticut; died 25 Feb 1978 Newport Beach, Orange, California. She married 3 Jul 1916, Detroit, Wayne, Michigan to **Nathan Alexander Gibson**, son of Walter McGill Gibson and of Mary Alice Campbell.

BURIAL:

Date: 27 Feb 1978
Place: Monrovia, Los Angeles, California

BIOGRAPHICAL NOTES:

Eloped with Nathaniel. Father was initially opposed to marriage because he expected her to take care of him as a proper German daughter should. Once he met Nathaniel, he changed his mind and "they made up."

Illustration B.9

I like to have the actual details of my documentation listed on the computer—1850 census, Saginaw County, Saginaw, Michigan, etc. In this way, when I share my genealogy, the people I send it to will have ready access to my sources.

There is the possibility of listing your sources in the notes for each individual, but this would detract from the program's unique biographical function. Source notes would seriously impede the flow of the narrative in your descendancy history.

A more serious weakness of EFT is that although it has the GED-COM feature, there is no provision for merging GEDCOM files with your master file. This means that if you were to find one of your ancestors in the Ancestral File data base at the Family History Center, you could copy that ancestor's pedigree, but when you went to add

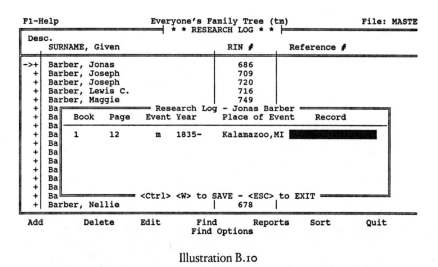

Illustration B.10

it automatically to your own pedigree, you would not be able to do so. The most you could do would be to create a subfile for that person. This means that the pedigree would not be merged with your main information and could not be included on any of the reports made from the master file.

Although the program provides the ancestor chart to go back on one surname line, it does not provide for a cascading pedigree print-out as PAF does. There is no way to print out your whole pedigree unless you do it page by page.

In addition to these two things, the big advantage that PAF has over EFT is the sorted reports. EFT only allows you to sort by surname, RIN, or reference number. PAF, if you recall, allows you to sort according to any information field: birth date, birthplace, burial place, etc.

In summary, this program is excellent for people who would like to print a genealogy (the proper name for a descendancy list) of their family. It gives great scope for creativity in the area of composition, but does not greatly aid the research process. It is easy to use, which is a definite plus, and, if you subscribe the Dollarhide filing system, it is an excellent organization tool.

The program retails for $169.00, which includes the GEDCOM utility. While this is considerably more than PAF, it is a lot less than the price of Roots III, which requires even more expensive add-on utilities to do the same things that EFT does.

A free demo disk is available from Dollarhide Systems, 203 West Holly Street, M4, Bellingham, WA 98225; 1-800-733-3807. Please indicate preference for 3½" or 5¼" disk.

III. Roots III

This is another very popular genealogy program for IBM and clones. It is extremely powerful and offers a variety of features that are not found in any other program. However, my own experience is that it is difficult to learn to use. I would not recommend it for computer novices. My husband is a sophisticated computer user who reviews software for the American Bar Association, and even he found it challenging to understand. It is his opinion that only those who are willing to invest the significant time and energy required to learn a complex program should attempt it. On the positive side, those who are experienced computer users, and who are of the Poirotian school of detection, will find the program fascinating and rewarding.

Because of the price, $249.95 (plus another $40.00 if you wish to add the GEDCOM utility), you might want to consider writing for the demo disk, which shows most of the applications of the program. It sells for ten dollars and is accompanied by a sample book displaying examples of printed reports. The address is COMMSOFT, 7795 Bell Road, P.O. Box 310, Windsor, CA 95492-0310; (707) 838-4300, (800) 327-6687.

The main differences between Roots and the other programs are its flexibility and the additional features that it offers. The promotional literature says "Roots III provides assistance on genealogical projects from the start of research to the printing of a formal book." The latter is only possible, however, if you purchase Roots Writer at an additional $45.00, whereas with EFT this feature is included in the base program.

Due to the preponderance of options available to the Roots user, the program is more difficult to move around in than either PAF or EFT, and unfortunately the tutorial is inadequate and confusing. The best way to learn to use it is to load the sample data file "Kennedy" and just explore, using the manual.

The template for adding an individual looks like Illustration B.11.

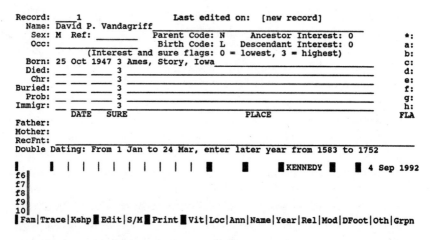

```
Record:      1              Last edited on:  [new record]
  Name: David P. Vandagriff_____
   Sex: M  Ref: _____   Parent Code: N    Ancestor Interest: 0        *:
   Occ: _____     Birth Code: L   Descendant Interest: 0        a:
            (Interest and sure flags: 0 = lowest, 3 = highest)           b:
  Born: 25 Oct 1947 3 Ames, Story, Iowa_____         c:
  Died: __ __ ___ 3 _____         d:
   Chr: __ __ ___ 3 _____         e:
Buried: __ __ ___ 3 _____         f:
  Prob: __ __ ___ 3 _____         g:
Immigr: __ __ ___ 3 _____         h:
            DATE    SURE                 PLACE                          FLA
Father:
Mother:
RecFnt:_____
Double Dating: From 1 Jan to 24 Mar, enter later year from 1583 to 1752
```

Illustration B.11

One of the great advantages of Roots over both PAF and EFT is that by pressing function keys you can change the event fields, so that different information can be recorded instead of what is initially shown. If you do not see an event listed that you wish to record, you may name your own. Some of the optional events are: baptism, birth, burial, bar mitzvah, census, christening, confirmation, death, divorce, divorce filing, employment, endowment (LDS), engagement, first communion, graduation, immigration, marriage, marriage banns, marriage contract, marriage license, marriage settlement, passenger list, probate of estate, residing, retirement, sealed to parents (LDS), sealed to spouse (LDS). From this list it is possible to produce 10,000 different combinations of events for any one person. It is also possible to enter a detailed footnote for each event, which makes documentation easier and more complete than with PAF and more accessible than with EFT.

Families are displayed on the screen, showing information added from event fields (Illustration B.12).

Roots refers to its focus and sort procedures as "grouping." There are eight ways in which you may group your data: by event or combination of events, by location, by date, by name, by detail/major footnote, by year range, by relationship, or by modification history. The last three categories are not available on PAF.

After grouping, you may print the following reports (those followed

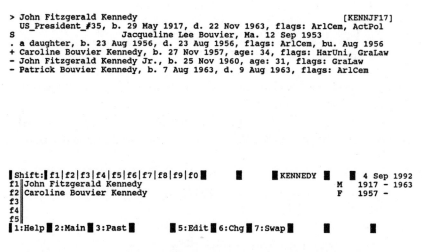

```
> John Fitzgerald Kennedy                                    [KENNJF17]
  US_President_#35, b. 29 May 1917, d. 22 Nov 1963, flags: ArlCem, ActPol
S                    Jacqueline Lee Bouvier, Ma. 12 Sep 1953
. a daughter, b. 23 Aug 1956, d. 23 Aug 1956, flags: ArlCem, bu. Aug 1956
+ Caroline Bouvier Kennedy, b. 27 Nov 1957, age: 34, flags: HarUni, GraLaw
- John Fitzgerald Kennedy Jr., b. 25 Nov 1960, age: 31, flags: GraLaw
- Patrick Bouvier Kennedy, b. 7 Aug 1963, d. 9 Aug 1963, flags: ArlCem
```

```
█Shift:█f1│f2│f3│f4│f5│f6│f7│f8│f9│f0█      █     █KENNEDY █   █ 4 Sep 1992
f1║John Fitzgerald Kennedy                              M   1917 - 1963
f2║Caroline Bouvier Kennedy                             F   1957 -
f3║
f4║
f5║
█1:Help█ 2:Main█ 3:Past█     █ 5:Edit█ 6:Chg█ 7:Swap█     █       █
```

Illustration B.12

by * are not available on PAF, those followed by ** not available on EFT):

Pedigree Chart
Family Group Sheet
Ahnentafel Chart
Descendant Chart
Genealogy Format (Register and Record Plan)*
Hereditary Statistics*,**
Individual List
Major Footnote List*,**
Marriage List**
Anniversary List**
Relationship List*,**
Summary Data*,**
Index*

An exciting feature of Roots is that these lists can be printed for specific groups. This feature can be used to print literally hundreds of customized reports to define and focus your data in virtually unlimited ways. Poirot would love it!

Register and Record Plan make it possible to prepare a formal family history without resorting to family group sheets and pedigree charts. They weave text into the report and provide both an index and a table of contents for up to 10,000 pages. These reports are very similar to those in EFT.

To summarize, Roots III targets those genealogists who are serious about using their data to create family histories, charts, and reports. It stores far more documentary data than PAF, thereby lessening your dependence on notes and documents. All the data can be printed out in specifically defined fashion to place in notebooks and aid research. In this way it is better than either of the previously reviewed programs.

However, Roots III is not a program for the novice. It would certainly frustrate any beginning computer user and possibly overwhelm any beginning genealogist.

If you have created a healthy pedigree and feel that you are sufficiently savvy to try Roots, you can transfer your data from one of the other programs to Roots using GEDCOM.

IV. Family Tree Maker

This program is popular among both novice genealogists and novice computer-users. While it doesn't have the power of the other three programs, it prints the most beautiful charts. Illustration B.13 shows the descendancy chart that can be printed out using Family Tree Maker. There are seven border styles to choose from, five box styles available to display individual information on charts, and each tree can be customized to include just the information you want. You can even include a short character description such as: "Was gentle with humans, animals, and all living things." The original kit contains twenty-five pieces of antique-finish parchment paper that can be used to create family history gifts or pages for your own book. These charts make an impressive presentation.

Another plus about this software is its ease of use. Of the four programs discussed here, I rate it as the most user-friendly. If programs could be said to have personalities, Family Tree Maker's would be grandmotherly and warm. The tutorial is excellent, aimed at the first-time computer user who is operating a system that is 100 percent IBM compatible. The tutorial takes less than an hour and teaches you to do all the basics, using a "card file system" as a template for entering names.

The templates are simple and nonthreatening. Illustration B.14 shows

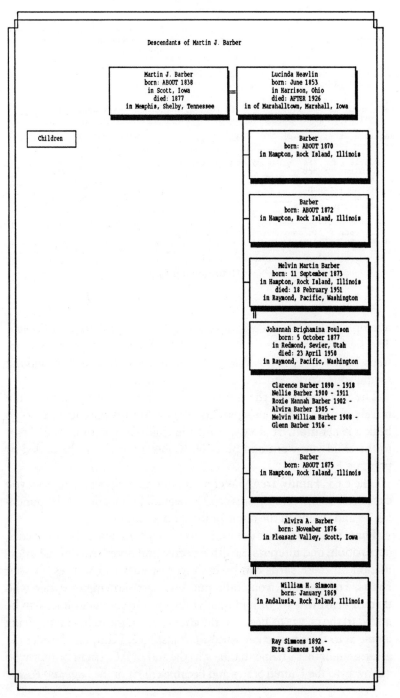

Descendants of Martin J. Barber

Martin J. Barber
born: ABOUT 1838
in Scott, Iowa
died: 1877
in Memphis, Shelby, Tennessee

Lucinda Heavlin
born: June 1853
in Harrison, Ohio
died: AFTER 1926
in of Marshalltown, Marshall, Iowa

Children

Barber
born: ABOUT 1870
in Hampton, Rock Island, Illinois

Barber
born: ABOUT 1872
in Hampton, Rock Island, Illinois

Melvin Martin Barber
born: 11 September 1873
in Hampton, Rock Island, Illinois
died: 18 February 1951
in Raymond, Pacific, Washington

Johannah Brighamina Poulson
born: 5 October 1877
in Redmond, Sevier, Utah
died: 23 April 1950
in Raymond, Pacific, Washington

Clarence Barber 1890 - 1918
Nellie Barber 1900 - 1911
Roxie Hannah Barber 1902 -
Alvira Barber 1905 -
Melvin William Barber 1908 -
Glenn Barber 1916 -

Barber
born: ABOUT 1875
in Hampton, Rock Island, Illinois

Alvira A. Barber
born: November 1876
in Pleasant Valley, Scott, Iowa

William H. Simmons
born: January 1869
in Andalusia, Rock Island, Illinois

Ray Simmons 1892 -
Etta Simmons 1900 -

Illustration B.13

```
        ┌───────────────┬─────────────┬───────────────┐
        │  F4 - Parents of │ F5 - Parents of │  F2 - Index   │
  Adolphus & Annis │     Annis    │   Adolphus   │   of names    │

Husband:   Adolphus  French _____
Date born: 8 Dec 1783_____ in Massachusetts_____
      died: 27 Apr 1850_____ in of Rock Island, Illinois_____

Wife:      Annis  Grinnells _____
Date born: 25 Apr 1789_____ in Leyden, Hampshire, Massachusetts_____
      died: 12 Dec 1831_____ in New York_____

Marriage date:      BEFORE 1804_____          Divorced:  N
Marriage location:  _____

        Children  [F6] - Family card of child    Sex     Birth dates
   1    Almira  French _____  F   15 Feb 1806_____
   2    Adolphus  French _____  M   20 Mar 1807_____
   3    Ethan  French _____  M   23 Mar 1808_____
   4    Laura L. French _____  F   7 Apr 1810_____
   5    Permelia  French _____  F   16 Jan 1812_____
                    More children
                                          Card: 1 2 3 4 M S P ^Q ^P
FOUND!  Press F7 to search again, or Esc to cancel.            1 of ?
F9-Menu   PgDn-Individ'l cards   F3-Other spouses   F7-Find individ'l   F1-Help
```

Illustration B.14

a template that has been completely filled out for Adolphus French. The save function is not as easy as PAF, however. It requires more steps, and makes it possible to go on to another function without saving your work, which could be frustrating.

The index tabs on the top of the card provide easy linking. You merely choose Adolphus's parents (F5) or Annis's parents (F4) to go back a generation. To do cards for the children, you move the cursor to the child you want and press F6. Other spouses can be added by pressing F3.

Like EFT, Family Tree Maker maintains an index of names that you can access at any time by pressing F2. Searching is made easy by punching F7 and typing in the name of the individual.

Three other file cards are available for each individual—for events, occupation, and interests; health records; and notes. Any of the information on these cards can be used to custom-create entries on your charts. For instance, you could make a chart showing everyone who died of heart disease or had mental illness. Or comment lines can be added to the charts to flesh out the characters of the individuals, giving a hint as to their particular voices. For instance, I could add under my great-grandfather's name that he was the son of a German printer who ran away to the United States and became editor of the *Saginaw Post*.

On the notes card, a word processor format is used that enables you to enter up to five pages of text. This gives you more scope, but unfortunately these notes only appear as a separate document when they are printed out. They are not integrated into the charts as in EFT or Roots.

Other features include a kinship function that will tell you how two people are related, and a calendar that will print out all the birth dates of a list of relatives. This can even include ages and length of marriage.

Compared to the other programs reviewed, this is probably the least helpful to the researching genealogist. It is excellent for primary organization functions, and its illustration capabilities make it the most creative desktop publisher of pedigree and decendancy charts. However, there isn't any provision for documentation, and manipulating data is not even an option. The only sorting function available is by name or birth date. As far as visualizing your family tree and moving around it from a pedigree chart, this can't be done. You can preview your print screens, but that is all. There is no provision for a cascading pedigree as in PAF or a descendancy with substantial text as in EFT. Also, though technically GEDCOM compatible, the GEDCOM file remains in a separate file from your main pedigree. As with EFT, there is no provision for merging them.

If you are primarily interested in producing a beautiful set of family charts, this is definitely the program for you. Family Tree Maker retails for $59.95, which is inexpensive enough that you could buy it along with another program and use it primarily for printing functions, transferring your data with GEDCOM. GEDCOM is not included in the basic package, but can be purchased for an additional $29.95 plus $2.00 for shipping and handling. The address is Banner Blue, P.O. Box 7865, Fremont, CA 94537.

As you can see, each of the above programs is designed for a different user. What kind are you? A Poirotian detective with excellent computer skills and a healthy pocketbook? Roots III is your program. EFT will be the choice of the more intuitive user with a flair for writing. What if you don't have a lot of time to spend on genealogy, but want your efforts to be showcased for the maximum impact? Try Family Tree Maker. As for Sherlock Holmes, he would undoubtedly prefer the straightforward, utilitarian approach of PAF.

APPENDIX C

Where to Get Genealogy Forms

1. Family History Center of the Church of Jesus Christ of Latter-day Saints. You can locate the one nearest you by calling the closest LDS church. A good time to call is on Sunday.

2. Everton Publishers. Telephone toll free 1-800-443-6325 for a catalogue. Everton is one of the largest genealogical supply companies in the country. Their catalogue includes everything from charts, forms, and binders to computer software and CD-ROM diskettes. Telephone or mail orders are accepted.

3. Local genealogical society in your county. Check with the local history section of your library for information.

4. A Latter-day Saint bookstore (sometimes listed as LDS Bookstore in the Yellow Pages).

APPENDIX D

Where to Find the Census

National Archives, Washington D.C.
  National Archives, branch offices:
    Boston, Massachusetts
    New York, New York
    Philadelphia, Pennsylvania
    Atlanta, Georgia
    Chicago, Illinois
    Kansas City, Missouri
    Fort Worth, Texas
    Denver, Colorado
    San Francisco, California
    Los Angeles, California
    Seattle, Washington
  National Archives Rental Program
  Wayne County Public Library, Fort Wayne, Indiana
  Mid-Continent Public Library, Independence, Missouri
  American Genealogical Lending Library, Bountiful, Utah
  Family History Library, Salt Lake City, Utah
  All branches of Family History Library

APPENDIX E

Sources for Colonial American
Immigration Records

Ames, Azel. *The Mayflower and Her Log: July 15, 1620–May 7, 1621*. Boston: Houghton, Mifflin & Co., 1901.

Banks, Charles Edward. *The English Ancestry and Homes of the Pilgrim Fathers*. Baltimore: The Genealogical Publishing Co., 1968.

———. *The Planters of the Commonwealth*. Baltimore: The Genealogical Publishing Co., 1967.

Brownwell, E. E., ed. *Topographical Dictionary of 2,885 English Emigrants to New England, 1620–1650*. Baltimore: The Genealogical Publishing Co., 1963.

Bridgers, Frank E., and Meredith B. Colket. *Guide to Genealogical Records in the National Archives*. Washington, D.C.: The National Archives, 1964.

———. *The Winthrop Fleet of 1630*. Baltimore: The Genealogical Publishing Co., 1963.

Egle, William Henry, ed. *Names of Foreigners Who Took the Oath of Allegience to the Province and State of Pennsylvania, 1727–1775, With the Foreign Arrivals, 1786–1808*. Baltimore: The Genealogical Publishing Co., 1967.

Emigrants from England, 1773–1776, and List of Emigrants to America from Liverpool, 1697–1707. Reprints from the *New England Historical and Genealogical Registers*, vols. 61, 64, and 65.

Farmer, John. *A Genealogical Register of the First Families of New England*. Baltimore: The Genealogical Publishing Co., 1968.

Faust, Albert Bernhardt. *List of Swiss Emigrants in the Eighteenth Century to the American Colonies*. Washington, D.C.: The National Genealogical Society, 1925.

Fothergill, Gerald. *Emigrants from England, 1773-1776*. Baltimore: The Genealogical Publishing Co., 1964.

———. *A List of Emigrant Ministers to America, 1690-1811*. Baltimore: The Genealogical Publishing Co., 1965.

French, Elizabeth. *List of Emigrants to America From Liverpool, 1697-1707*. Baltimore: The Genealogical Publishing Co., 1962.

Gerber, Adolph. *Emigrants From Wuerttemberg: The Adolph Gerber Lists*. Edited by Donald Herbert Yoder. Baltimore: The Genealogical Publishing Co., n.d.

Ghirelli, Michael. *List of Emigrants from England to America, 1682-1692*. Baltimore: Magna Carta Book Co., 1968.

Greer, George Cabell. *Early Virginia Immigrants, 1623-1666*. Baltimore: The Genealogical Publishing Co., 1960.

Hansen, Marcus Lee. *The Atlantic Migration, 1607-1860*. New York: Harper & Row, 1961.

Hoffman, William J. "Palatine Emigrants to America from the Principality of Nassau-Dillenburg." *The National Genealogical Society Quarterly*, vol. 30 (June 1941): 41-44.

Hotten, John Camden. *The Original Lists of Person of Quality, 1600-1700*. Second edition. Baltimore: The Genealogical Publishing Co., 1968.

Ireland, Gordon. "Servants of Foreign Plantations from Bristol, England 1654-1686." *New York Genealogical and Biographical Record*, vol. 79 (1948): 65-75.

Jewson, Charles Boardman. *Transcript of Three Registers of Passengers from Great Yarmouth to Holland and New England, 1637-1639*. Baltimore: The Genealogic al Publishing Co., 1964.

Kaminkow, Jack, and Marion Kaminkow. *A List of Emigrants From England to America, 1718-1759*. Baltimore: The Genealogical Publishing Co., 1964.

Knittle, Walter Allen. *Early Eighteenth Century Palatine Emigration*. Baltimore: The Genealogical Publishing Co., 1965.

Krebs, Friedrich. "Emigrants from Baden-Durlach to Pennsylvania, 1749-1755." *The National Genealogical Society Quarterly*, vol. 45 (March 1957): 30-32.

———. "A List of German Immigrants to the American Colonies from Zweibruecken in the Palatinate, 1756-1771." *Pennsylvania German Folklore Society*, vol. 16 (1951): 171-83.

Lancour, Harold. *A Bibliography of Ship Passenger Lists, 1538–1825.* Third edition. New York: The New York Public Library, 1963.

Landis, John T. *Mayflower Descendants and their Marriages for Two Generations after Landing.* Baltimore: The Genealogical Publishing Co., 1964.

Myers, Albert Cook. *Quaker Arrivals At Philadelphia, 1682–1750.* Baltimore: The Genealogical Publishing Co., 1969.

Nicholson, Cregoe, D.P. *Some Early Emigrants to America.* Baltimore: The Genealogical Publishing Co., 1965.

"A Partial List of the Families Who Arrived at Philadelphia Between 1682 and 1687." *The Pennsylvania Magazine of History and Biography*, vol. 8 (1884): 255–58.

"Passenger List of the Ship 'Elizabeth' Which Arrived at Philadelphia, Pennsylvania, 1819." *The Pennsylvania Magazine of History and Biography*, vol. 25 (1901): 255–58.

Putnam, Eben. *Two Early Passenger Lists, 1635–1637.* Baltimore: The Genealogical Publishing Co., 1964.

Revill, Janie. *A Compliation of the Original Lists of Protestant Immigrants to South Carolina, 1763–1773.* Baltimore: The Genealogical Publishing Co., 1968.

Robinson, Conway. *Early Voyages to America.* Richmond: Sheperd & Colin, 1848.

Rupp, Israel Daniel. *A Collection of Upwards of Thirty Thousand Names of German, Swiss, Dutch, French and Other Immigrants into Pennsylvania From 1727–1776.* Second edition. Baltimore: The Genealogical Publishing Co., 1965.

Sherwood, George. *American Colonists in English Records.* Baltimore: The Genealogical Publishing Co., 1969.

Standard, William G. *Some Emigrants to Virginia.* Second edition. Baltimore: The Genealogical Publishing Co., 1964.

Steinemann, Ernst, ed. "A List of Eighteenth Century Emigrants from the Canton of Schaffhausen to the American Colonies, 1734–1752." *The Pennsylvania German Folklore Society*, vol. 16 (1951): 185–96.

Strassburger, Ralph Beaver, and William John Hinke, eds. *Pennsylvania German Pioneers: A Publication of the Original Lists of Arrivals in the Port of Philadelphia From 1727–1808.* Two volumes. Baltimore: The Genealogical Publishing Co., 1966.

Virginia Historical Society. *Documents Relating to the Huguenot Emigration to Virginia.* Richmond: The Virginia Historical Society, 1936.

Virkus, Frederick A. *Immigrant Ancestors: A List of 2,500 Immigrants to America Before 1750.* Baltimore: The Genealogical Publishing Co., 1963.

Westcott, Thompson. *Names of Persons Who Took the Oath of Allegiance to the State of Pennsylvania Between the Years 1777 and 1789.* Baltimore: The Genealogical Publishing Co., 1963.

About the Author

G.G. Vandagriff lives in the Missouri Ozarks with her husband and three children. She has worked as a genealogy librarian in her local Family History Center since 1987, helping people of all backgrounds trace their ancestors.

A former college instructor in economics with a Master's in International Relations, Vandagriff now gives family history workshops. Anyone interested in hosting a workshop should contact her at:

Voices in Your Blood Workshop
P.O. Box 187
Monett, MO 65708

Bibliography

Bremer, Ronald A. *Compendium of Historical Sources*. Salt Lake City: Progenitor Genealogical Society, Inc., 1983.

Bruce, Dwight H. *Onondaga's Centenniel: Gleanings of a Century*. Boston: Boston History Company, 1896.

Cerney, John, and Arlene Eakle, eds. *The Source, A Guidebook of American Genealogy*. Salt Lake City: Ancestry Publishing Company, 1984.

Clayton, Dr. W.W. *History of Onondaga County, New York*. Syracuse: D. Mason & Co., 1878.

Conroy, Cathryn. "Building a Generation Map." *CompuServe Magazine*. July 1992.

Covey, Stephen R. *The Seven Habits of Highly Effective People: Powerful Lessons in Personal Change*. New York: Simon & Schuster, 1990.

Dickinson, Emily. "I Never Saw a Moor." *A Pocket Book of Modern Verse*. Oscar Williams, ed. New York: Washington Square Press, 1954.

Dollarhide, William, ed. *Genealogy Bulletin*. Number 13 (January, February, March 1992). Bellingham, Washington: Dollarhide Systems, 1992.

———. *Managing a Genealogical Project*. Baltimore: Genealogical Publishing Company, Inc., 1988.

Doyle, Sir Arthur Conan. "The Sign of the Four." *The Complete Sherlock Holmes*. New York: Doubleday, 1930.

Ellis, Havelock. *The Dance of Life*. Boston: Houghton Mifflin Company, 1923.

Family History Memorandum. Vol. 13. no. 2. Salt Lake City: Family History Center.

Goleman, Daniel, Paul Kaufman, and Michael Ray. *The Creative Spirit*. New York: Dutton, 1992.

Gouldrup, Lawrence P., Ph.D. *Writing the Family Narrative*. Ancestry, Inc., 1987.

History of Kalamazoo, Michigan. Philadelphia: Everts & Abbot, 1880.

Joyce, James. *Portrait of the Artist as a Young Man*. New York: Viking Press, 1944.

Llewellyn, Richard. *How Green Was My Valley*. New York: The Macmillan Co., 1940.

Massie, Larry B., and Peter J. Schmit. *Kalamazoo: The Place Behind the Products*. Kalamazoo: Windsor Publications, 1981.

Masters, Edgar Lee. *Spoon River Anthology*. New York: Collier Macmillan Publishers, 1962.

Moore, Floyd Wayne. *Kalamazoo, Michigan: The Evolution of a Modern City*. Ph.D. dissertation, Northwestern University, 1941.

Redford, Dorothy Spruill. *Somerset Homecoming: Recovering a Lost Heritage*. New York: Doubleday, 1988.

Smith, Caroll E. *Pioneer Times in Onondaga County*. Syracuse: C. W. Bardeen, 1904.

Somogyi, Barbara, and David Stanton. "Amy Tan: An Interview." *Poets and Writers' Magazine*. September/October, 1991.

The Handybook for Genealogists. Eighth edition. Logan, Utah: The Everton Publishers, Inc., 1991.

Thomas, Lewis. *The Lives of a Cell*. New York: Viking Press, 1974.

Toqueville, Alexis de. *Democracy in America*. Richard D. Heffner, ed. New York: New American Library, 1956.

Ulrich, Laurel Thatcher. *A Midwife's Tale*. New York: Vintage, 1990.

U.S. Department of Health and Human Services. *Where to Write for Vital Records*. Hyattsville, Maryland, 1990.

Walker, Alice. Review of *Somerset Homecoming* on jacket of same.

Wilbour, Benjamin Franklin. *Little Compton Families*. Little Compton, Rhode Island: Little Compton Historical Society, 1967.

Wilder, Thornton. *Our Town*. New York: Harper & Row, 1938.

———. *The Bridge of San Luis Rey*. New York: Avon Books, 1928.

Wright, Norman E. *Building An American Pedigree*. Provo, Utah: Brigham Young University Press, 1974.

Index

Action steps: research, 22
American Historical Society of Germans from Russia, 89
Ancestral File: about 52–56; submissions to, 56; submitters, 55; using GEDCOM with, 54
Ancestors: cause and effect in their lives, 112; conflict in their lives, 113; psychological and historical perspective, 106–12

Biographical sheets: examples, 36, 104

Cemetery indexes: where to find, 32, 66
Census: 1880–1920, 43–50; 1850–1870, 39–43; how to use, 37–50; index, 41–42; purpose of, 38; 1790–1840, 43–45; Soundex, 45–46; where to find, 38–39, 41, 159
Church records: where to find, 32
City histories: where to find, 33
Civil War records, 80–85
CompuServe, 79
Computer software for genealogists, 16, 141–57
Conflict in ancestor's life, 113
Country of origin, using census to find, 49
County history: as source for biography, 109; where to find, 33, 66
County records: obtaining by correspondence, 26–31; to search in person, 30

Documentation, maintaining records, 17

Dollarhide, William: *Managing a Genealogical Project,* 20
Dollarhide systems, 21

Enumeration district, census 46–47
Everyone's Family Tree, 146–51

Family group sheet, about, 17
Family histories: how to write, 107–15; where to find, 34
Family History Centers: how to find, 52; resources in, 51–71; using to obtain country records, 30
Family History Library Catalog: Locality Browse, 64; Locality Search, 65; menu, 65; Surname Search, 67–71
Family organizations, 74
Family registry, 74
Family search: about, 52–71; Ancestral File, 52–56; International Genealogical Index, 56–59; Family History Library Catalog, 64–71; Military Index, 60; Social Security Death Index, 59
Family Tree Maker, 154–157

GEDCOM: in genealogy software, 141; using to submit to Ancestral File, 56; using with Ancestral File, 54
Genealogical Helper: source for ethnic societies, 89; using for surname research, 75–76; using to find family organizations, 74; using to hire researcher, 67
Genealogical societies: correspondence with, 31–36; sources for, 31